A Spirited War

George Washington and the Ghosts of the Revolution in Central New Jersey

by Donald Johnstone Peck

Flying Camp Press

An Imprint of
American History Imprints
Franklin, Tennessee
1-888-521-1789

AMERICAN
HISTORY
IMPRINTS

For this and other fine American history titles, please visit us on the Internet:

www.Americanhistoryimprints.com

Book interior and cover design by Gordon Bond
Front and back cover artwork "George Washington at Market Square, Perth Amboy, New Jersey" from an original painting by Francis J. McGinley. Used with the permission of the artist.

ISBN 13: 978-0-9842256-2-0
ISBN 10: 0-9842256-2-5

First Edition November 2009
Library of Congress Control Number: 2009938285

Printed in the United States of America on acid-free paper
This book meets all ANSI standards for archival quality.

Dedicated to
MY LONGTIME COMPANION
JAMES P. EGAN

and

THE DIRECTORS OF THE
RARITAN-MILLSTONE HERITAGE ALLIANCE

CLASS OF 2004
GEORGE B. DAWSON
The Reverend BRUCE FREEMAN
MARILYN W. RAUTIO
ANN M. SUYDAM
The Reverend EVERETT L. ZABRISKIE III

CLASS OF 2005
MICHAEL BOYLAN
MARJORIE V. KLER FREEMAN
BONITA KRAFT GRANT
SARAH ISRAEL
PAUL JENNINGS, M.D.
CAROL CLEVELAND NATARELLI
CONSTANCE M. O'GRADY

CLASS OF 2006
JOHN F. ALLEN
PAULA HENRY
PETER A. PRIMAVERA
ELIZABETH SCOTT
MARJORIE WATSON
KATHLEEN WILLIAMSON

IN MEMORIAM
ISABELLA ELLIS CARTER PECK
GLADYS ESTELLE PECK JOHNSON
The Reverend WILLIAM M. JUSTICE
Professor D. ELTON TRUEBLOOD
The Reverend JOHN STANLEY GRAUEL
The Reverend Canon GEORGE H. BOYD
LORETTA GALVIN LEWIS
Colonel C. MALCOLM B. GILMAN, M.D.

Contents

Part One **Divided Loyalties**

Part Two **Defeat, Retreat & Victory**

Part Three **Geography, History & Culture**

Part Four **Headquarters of the Generals**

Part Five **His Excellency, George Washington**

Acknowledgements

$\mathcal{I}$ acknowledge the help and encouragement of the following individuals: James G. Anderton, Alan I. Appelbaum, Judith G. Beam, France-Aimee Beekman, Richard V. Bialo, Robert F. Brown, Gwendolyn Compton, Joel Carver Compton, Alma Geist Cap, Judith Cronin, Marjorie V. Kler Freeman, Bonita Kraft Grant, Joyce Harrison, Beau James, Richard A. Johnson, Sr., Donna M. Kabay, Susan C. Keating, Doris Baker Kersten, Thorton B. Lounsbury, William F. Lynch, Janice Peck Margolis, Theodore J. Miller, Albert E. Mussad, Ph.D. Carol C. Natarelli, George E. Pirocchi, Jr., Elizabeth S. Pittenger, Albert M. Previte, Joanne Price, Charles S. Rall, Robert A. Ratigan, Christine A. Retz, B. Preston Root, III, Norman S. Rosen, Brynne Johnson Solowinski, Doris R. Stauderman, Dee Von Suskil, Robert Carre Turner, and Evelyn V. Waller.

Others gave me needed assistance with the chapters that follow: Historic Perth Amboy: Kathleen Manning DePow; Proprietary House: Willard Sterne Randall, Richard Spencer Perry and Joanne Kaiser; Historic Indian Queen Tavern: Marjorie V. Kler Freeman, Anna M. Aschkenes, Jack D. Stine and Linda McTeague; The Conference House: Lee Conti and the Reverend J. Rodney Croes of St. Peter's Church, Perth Amboy; New Jersey's Darkest Hour: the Reverend Dr. David Davis of the Nassau Presbyterian Church, Princeton; Morven and the Old Stockton Family: Martha Leigh Wolf and Deborah Kashar; The Triumph In New Jersey Of Courage And Conviction: John K. Mills; Washington Rock: George Stillman, Sr. and David M. Flynn; Olde Stone Cottage at Cutter Farm: Brynne Johnson Solowinski; The Monmouth: David G. Martin, John D.

Katerba, Hara Durkin and June Sadlowski; Wallace House: James Kurzenberger; Jacobus Vanderveer House, Ellen Vreeland, and Jack D. Stine; Abraham Staats House: Kathleen Faulks and Marilyn Rautio; Rockingham: John and Nancy Allen and Lisa Flick; Historic Cross Keys Tavern: Joseph and Desty Rauch , Jeffery Huber and Barbara Wyatt.

My final acknowledgements are to my friends, C. Robert Kochek and Lee E. Nordholm who read the manuscript for accuracy, and Lee E. Nordholm and Gordon Bond who created the layouts for the book. My thanks also to David E. Kane, the publisher, whose final editing is much appreciated. A special thanks goes to the Board of Directors of the Raritan-Millstone Heritage Alliance, Inc., its members and sites, and especially its former President, Peter A. Primavera and Vice President, Ann M. Suydam, for the work they have done to promote, protect and preserve the historical, cultural and environmental sites within the greater region of the Raritan and Millstone River systems.

Donald Johnstone Peck

Preface

More than eighty-two years after the first Independence Day was celebrated in New Brunswick, New Jersey on July 4, 1778, Abraham Lincoln, in his address to the Senate of the State of New Jersey, said, "I cannot but remember the place New Jersey holds in the early struggle of our country. I remember that in the revolutionary struggle none had more of its battlefields. I remember reading in my youth a small book–the life of Washington–and of all of his struggles none fixed itself on my mind so indelibly, as the crossing of the Delaware, preceding the battle of Trenton. I remember that these great struggles were made for some object. I am exceedingly anxious that the object they fought for–liberty, and the Union and Constitution they formed–shall be perpetual."

Lincoln's basic summary of New Jersey's colonial history and critical role in winning the American Revolution was similar to that of many people, even though his own great-great-great grandparents-Mordecai Lincoln and Hannah Salter-were from Monmouth County, New Jersey.

Today, New Jersey, as the Crossroads of the American Revolution, is finally being recognized for its historic, cultural, and environmental importance in winning the War for Independence. Central Jersey, particularly Middlesex, Somerset, Monmouth and Mercer Counties, and those areas through which the Raritan and Millstone Rivers and their tributaries flow, has a rich, eventful, and unique heritage that played a significant role in the founding of the United States. My interest in the colonial and Revolutionary events of New Jersey–incidents that have shaped our nation's heritage from its earliest beginnings–was prompted by my upbringing in historic Woodbridge. As a boy, I explored the ancient 1707 Quaker graveyard that once surrounded the old United Methodist Church Parsonage, built on the earlier stone foundations of the 1713 Quaker Meeting House on Main Street. I gazed at the early gravestones of Woodbridge settlers and patriots found in the burying grounds of the Old White Church on Rahway Avenue, and mused about George Washington's historic visit to the Cross Keys Tavern.

Later, while a student at the University of Paris Institute of Political Studies, I traveled extensively throughout England and Europe, and enjoyed many in-depth visits to Italy, Greece, Israel, and Egypt. My interest in antiquities and the influence of culture on local history grew more intense.

As a young gentleman farmer at Cwm Rhondda Farm in Colts Neck, Monmouth County, I immersed myself in local history, contributing to the History of Colts Neck published in 1964 for the tercentenary of New Jersey.

However, it was not until I came face to face with the rich colonial history of Perth Amboy and that of my ancestors there, while a ninth generation resident in 1972, that I became active in the Proprietary House Association. As a life member, I served as Trustee for eighteen years and President for three nonconsecutive terms, and am presently President Emeritus.

Central New Jersey's crucial role as the Crossroads of the American Revolution became even more evident to me when I began serving as a Director of the Raritan-Millstone Heritage Alliance in 2004, and while President in 2007. The almost endless list of historic sites along the river valleys in the counties of Middlesex, Somerset, Monmouth and Mercer made it clear to me that the rich story of our American heritage, as interpreted through its sites and landscape, should be retold to a broader audience.

As a student of history, I quickly learned that the past is subject to interpretation. What happened in these four counties and the surrounding countryside is not readily obvious to the uneducated eye. It needed to be explained and promoted by those who deeply cared about its preservation. What I soon discovered was that no other geographic area could compare in telling the story of how the American Revolution was won, or the sacrifices that were made, to ensure its eventual success.

As one person, what could I do to motivate the broader public to become interested and engaged in Central New Jersey history? I found a partial answer in the work I had done as President of the Proprietary House Association. As part of my duties, I had scheduled appearances by the celebrated psychic, Jane Doherty, during our annual ghost tours, and for years Jane and I lead the tours. Jane would talk about the resident ghosts and I would talk about the history of the Proprietary House. Hundreds of people, far more than would come to visit the mansion when it was opened only on Wednesdays, showed up to enjoy a visit. They asked questions about the mansion and its history while touching its walls and furnishings, absorbing the past in all its forms. In fact, many people returned year after year, often bringing friends and relatives with them, learning by seeing, listening and touching what they may not have learned by reading. I concluded that my experience at the Proprietary House would work also at other historic sites.

The reader will shortly discover that I chose to receive Jane's assistance at many of the historic sites mentioned in this book. While this is an unusual methodology, to be sure, I feel that there is mystery to be uncovered, mystery not recorded in dusty history books sitting on library shelves. I personally accompanied Jane Doherty on all of her investigations, and duly recorded her findings, in order to interest readers in following in our footsteps, driving over the same crossroads that we traversed, and discovering for themselves the almost indescribable richness, beauty and intrigue that these Jersey Midlands have to offer-unique in our nation's history.

Donald Johnstone Peck
Olde Stone Cottage
Fords, New Jersey
November 2009

Foreword

*D*onald Johnstone Peck and his associate, Jane Doherty, have given us a fascinating and utterly new view of the Revolutionary War. Although dramatic actions occurred in other colonies–such as the Battles of Lexington and Concord and Bunker Hill in Massachusetts, and Ticonderoga and Saratoga in New York State, and Yorktown in Virginia–and although Washington's army famously suffered at Brandywine and through the long winter at Valley Forge–few Americans realize that Washington and the Continental Army spent more time in New Jersey than in any other state. And fewer still know the details of Washington's retreat across New Jersey in 1776, his return to win the Battles of Trenton and Princeton in 1776-7, his pursuit of the British at the great Battle of Monmouth in 1778, his survival at Morristown in the coldest winter of the century in 1779-80, the crucial battles of Springfield in June 1780, and of his march to victory with the French, led by the Comte de Rochambeau, in 1781. Peck and Doherty tell us the stories of these events through the eyes of those who were there, on the landscape of Central New Jersey. Peck–the historian–and Doherty–the psychic–traveled together to a dozen important historic sites in New Jersey and to one site a few miles from New Jersey on Staten Island, New York. Peck tells what historians believe happened at each site, and Doherty gives her impressions, her feelings, and her sensations, as she stands where people lived, worked, and died more than two centuries ago. Their tale is well told, and it is an exciting one. So read on, with pleasure.

George J. Hill, M.D., D. Litt.

Part One

Divided Loyalties

The Proprietary House

Historic Perth Amboy: History and Mystery

Mystery shrouds the long history of the venerable port city of Perth Amboy, reminding us that all circumstances are temporary. As in any historical investigation, one needs to search for hidden clues to unravel the fascinating stories of the past. Founded in 1683 by the Proprietors of the Province of East Jersey, Perth Amboy was described by one of them as a "sweet, wholesome and delightful place." Named for the Earl of Perth, Scotland, it became the capital of the first successful Scottish colony in North America. When he first viewed Perth Amboy, William Penn described it as the "garden on the earth most like to Paradise." In fact, at one point, he had seriously considered establishing his City of Brotherly Love here.

After being selected by the Proprietors, Robert Barclay of Scotland received the right to govern East Jersey for life from King Charles II, without the requirement of residence in the province. He served as governor from 1683-1690. The pattern of the streets and property lots of old Perth Amboy still follows Barclay's original survey map of 1684. Laid out on about 200 acres of "Ambo Point," it was the first known plan of an American city drawn up in the New World. The Native Americans called Amboy Point Ompo or Ompoye, meaning elbow. This soon became anglicized to *Ambo* or *Amboy* on the tongues of the English and Scottish settlers. The map is considered significant because of its extreme importance in understanding Perth Amboy and the role the city played in the development of East Jersey. A copy of this map is in the collection of the Proprietary House Association.

In 1676, Governor Barclay, considered the most prominent Quaker apologist of his day, wrote a religious treatise titled *An Apology for the True*

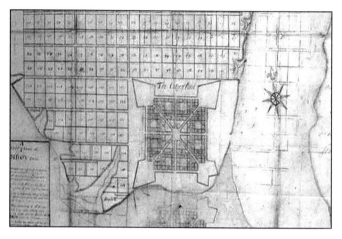

Perth Amboy's modern street plan still follows the patterns established by Robert Barclay in 1684. This survey represents the first known mapping of a town in North America.

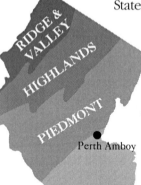

Christian. He is credited by his biographer, D. Elton Trueblood, for having saved Quakerism from extinction.

Approaching the city of Perth Amboy from Route 9 South, Jane Doherty and I drove under the Garden State Parkway and Route 9 bridges that span the Raritan River, and continued east on Smith Street, the city's main thoroughfare. As we reached the heights of the Keasbey area, Jane commented on our extended view of the river and the bay. "What you're seeing is only 10,000 years old!" I commented with irony. Uncertain as to what my remark meant, Jane asked me to explain. "Geology is always underfoot and taken for granted by most of us," I responded.

During the Pleistocene epoch of the Ice Age, the most recent geological event to alter New Jersey's topography was the Wisconsin ice advance, which began about 80,000 years ago. The ice was between 2,500 and 3,500 feet thick at its maximum. As the great ice sheet moved southward, the leading edge of the glacier acted like a giant bulldozer, pushing and scraping the ground in front of it. As the glacier advanced, huge boulders became rounded from friction and contact as they rolled along on the bottom. The advancing ice pack finally slowed to a stop, leaving an irregular line that terminated across north-central New Jersey. Its edge extended from Perth Amboy to Metuchen, north to Summit and west to Belvidere, leaving behind what is now called the Wisconsin terminal moraine, a wall of ice estimated to be 300 feet high. The Raritan River and Bay were nonexistent until the ice eventually melted and receded north.

Here, under the terminal moraine in Perth Amboy, is the northeast tip of New Jersey's Inner Coastal Plain, which began forming more than 100 million years ago, producing the sands, clays, and marls so common to the area. The clay beds provided the raw materials for the bricks and terra cotta for which Perth Amboy was so well known during the late nineteenth and early twentieth centuries.

No known portraits of Henry Hudson exist. This representation is from *Cyclopaedia of Universal History*, published in 1885.

The Wisconsin terminal moraine shaped the promontory that characterizes the city's boundaries between the Raritan River and the Arthur Kill (first called *Achter Col* (after bay) in Dutch, by Henry Hudson in 1609 because it lay behind New York Bay). It was this favorable location, opening onto Raritan Bay, which first attracted the original settlers from Scotland.

As we descended the Keasbey bluff on Smith Street into Perth Amboy, I pointed out that the Raritan Bay Union, a nineteenth century utopian cooperative community sited on 225 acres, once existed to our left. The Union attracted many famous antebellum abolitionists, artists and intellectuals such as Henry David Thoreau, William Cullen Bryant, Horace Greeley, Louis Comfort Tiffany, Ralph Waldo Emerson and others. Former Liberty Party presidential candidate, James G. Birney (1792-1857), was also a visitor to the Union.

Celebrated as art center from 1861-1876, the Raritan Bay Union was the residence of George Inness, one of America's leading painters. The Inness House, a stone house studio on the grounds, was destroyed in the late

The Prince of Wales just prior to his accession to the throne. At eighteen-years-old, he had visited Perth Amboy and later paid his respects at the tomb of George Washington. This photo was taken by W. & D. Downey, London photographers.

American landscape artist George Inness was among the artists to take up residence in Perth Amboy's Raritan Bay Union. This photo was taken 1890 by E. S. Bennett.

twentieth century. It was the last remaining physical vestige of this cultural utopia. Among other well-known utopias of the period were Ripley's "Brook Farm" and Alcott's "Fruitlands," both in New England, and the "North American Phalanx," in Colts Neck, New Jersey.

In 1860, at the age of eighteen, His Royal Highness the Prince of Wales (later King Edward VII), had visited this city when he sailed from Perth Amboy for New York City on the steamer *Harriet Lane*. Received at the White House by President James Buchanan and his niece Harriet Lane, the Prince later stood bareheaded at the tomb of George Washington while a marine band played a dirge from "Il Trovatore." The report that a direct descendant of King George III had honored the grave of the first American President converted the last of the skeptics of a rapprochement with Great Britain.

"I had no idea that Perth Amboy had so much to offer," Jane commented. At this point, all I could add was "Just wait and see! You're about to visit four centuries in one afternoon!"

We followed Smith Street through the central business district until we came to the waterfront. Here we viewed the oldest wooden ferry slip in the United States–the Perth Amboy-Tottenville Ferry Slip–at the site of the original Town Wharf. While ferry service from the foot of Fayette Street (originally named South Dock Street) to Staten Island dates back to 1684, the Smith Street ferry slip dates to 1867. After being closed in 1963, the slip was restored in 1998 to its 1904 appearance.

The oldest wooden ferry slip in the U.S., the Perth Amboy-Tottenville building was restored in 1998.

It was here that, as a lad of seventeen, the great patriot Benjamin Franklin crossed the Arthur Kill to Perth Amboy to board the Long Ferry from the foot of High Street to South Amboy. From there he walked the sixty miles across New Jersey to Burlington, and took another ferry to Philadelphia. Ghosts are reported to still stroll through Perth Amboy, clad in eighteenth century garb, as they are reputed to have done even before Benjamin Franklin first arrived here in 1723.

Benjamin Franklin entered New Jersey at Perth Amboy before trekking across the state en route to Philadelphia. H. B. Hall created this engraving from the original painted from life by J.A. Duplessis in 1783.

The great days of Perth Amboy's role as a seaport are long finished. The waterside streets that had once thronged with ships in wharves have all passed away. Gone are the famous inns, and the Long Ferry and King's Arms Taverns, where the old salts, fishermen and pilots gathered to tell their flock numerous tales, each no doubt better than the last.

As we drove over the quiet streets of this historic urban city, there remained a hush of recognition of earlier generations of this southern section of the city. Still in evidence were the carefully laid out 1684 streets and property lots of the Proprietors of East Jersey. Gone, however, are the grand mansions that stood on Water Street and High Street as tangible signs of a wealthy culture built on Oriental spoils brought home by navigators, naval heroes, and merchants. One of these sailors was the famous Commodore Lawrence Kearny, who was responsible for initiating the "Open Door" policy with China in 1842. His modest residence, circa 1780, still stands on Catalpa Avenue.

The demography of the colonial capital of Perth Amboy (1683-1790) was much like that of other provincial cities. Three distinct social classes developed: first, an aristocracy based on wealth, made up of the great landowners, the Proprietors; second, the independent farmers, skilled workers, small shopkeepers, and laborers; and third the indentured servants and African slaves. Here officers of the Crown mingled with local merchants who had grown rich

Commodore Lawrence Keary's Perth Amboy home is still standing.

while trading with the other North American colonies and the West Indies. Many of them lived in elegant houses staffed by numerous African slaves and attended the services of the Church of England, St. Peter's Church.

Like the giant English elms of this East Jersey capital, only a few of the important sites of the golden years of the city remain. Among these are the City Hall, formerly the Colonial and State Capitol Building, constructed circa 1713-14. It is the oldest public building in continuous use in the United States. It was here that New Jersey became the third state (after Delaware and Pennsylvania) to ratify the U.S. Constitution in 1787, and the first state to ratify the Bill of Rights, enumerating our individual freedoms, on November 20, 1789. In a municipal referendum, the first African American voter in the United States, Thomas Mundy Peterson, cast his ballot here on March 31, 1870, the day following the adoption of the Fifteenth Amendment to the U.S. Constitution.

Peterson was born a free man in Metuchen in 1824. His mother, Lucy Green, was born in Monmouth County. As a young boy, Peterson and his family moved to Perth Amboy. Here he married Daphne Reeve, whose parents had been slaves on an estate in Perth Amboy. Passing a ballot to an electioneer at historic City Hall, Peterson symbolically carried the first torch to be passed in what would become a long race for African American political liberation in this country.

Long since demolished are

Thomas Mundy Peterson, a school janitor in Perth Amboy, became the first African-American to vote under the 15th Amendment. The town later commemorated the event by presenting him with a gold medal on May 30, 1884. It can be seen pinned to his coat below. The school he worked at was later renamed in his honor and March 31st is considered "Thomas Mundy Peterson Day" in New Jersey.

Photograph courtesy the Perth Amboy Public Library.

the great mansions of the aristocrats with whom Royal Governor William and Lady Franklin socialized: the Johnstones, Kearnys, Parkers and Skinners. During and after the Revolution their homes were destroyed, as was nine-tenths of the city, by Tories and patriots alike. Even the Proprietary House could not escape a disastrous fire in 1786, which came close to leveling it. The Parker Castle, whose stone section was constructed by Scottish stonemasons in 1690, and which had been home to eight generations of the illustrious Parker family, was finally torn down in the twentieth century to make way for an apartment complex.

During the American Revolution, Perth Amboy was a hub for Loyalist activity. It also served as a permanent garrison for British troops in 1776 and 1777. Among Perth Amboy notables in the seventeenth and eighteenth centuries were George Keith, a theologian and surveyor, who surveyed the dividing line between East and West Jersey in 1687, known as Keith's Line. Others included Proprietor Dr. John Johnstone, member of the King's Council (1686-88 and 1704-26), Mayor of the City of New York (1714-18), Speaker of the New Jersey Provincial Assembly for ten years, and first in the list of men to whom Perth Amboy's Charter was given in 1718. Other residents were John Watson, the first American portrait painter; William Dunlap, a painter, first American playwright, and father of American drama, who painted George Washington at his Rockingham Headquarters in 1783; the Reverend Robert McKean, who founded the New Jersey Medical Society, the oldest medical association in America, and the nineteenth century resident William Adee Whitehead, author of *Contributions to the Early History of*

Born in Newark, N.J., Aaron Burr, Jr. served courageously during Benedict Arnold's assault on Quebec during the Revolution. He would also serve the new nation as New York's Senator and State Attorney General before becoming Vice President under Thomas Jefferson. He is best known, however, for his duel with Alexander Hamilton. After killing Hamilton, Burr fled to Perth Amboy.

Perth Amboy and Adjoining Country with Sketches of Men and Events in New Jersey During the Provincial Era. In addition, Aaron Burr, Jr. fled to this city after his famous duel with Alexander Hamilton, and stayed overnight at the Commodore Thomas Truxton House (called "Pleasant View") at 129 Water Street.

Perth Amboy has also been home to many early Provincial Governors whose residences no longer remain: Robert Hunter, William Burnet, John Hamilton, Francis Bernard and Thomas Boone.

As we approached the Proprietary House, the weather suddenly changed. A sea fog rolled in along the coast and hung like a pall over the old colonial section of the city. Foghorns could be heard out on the bay, warning ships of the nearby treacherous shoals. It had evolved into a lonesome, dreary day. I thought of those who, during the 325 years of history in this city, had preceded us and enriched our lives. Men and women who gave much more than they ever took from society, whose rewards we now enjoy. Looking up at the imposing edifice (the only royal governor's residence of which any portion remains in the original thirteen colonies), we were about to investigate a stage of events as full of human interest as any gray European feudal castle.

The Proprietors of East Jersey had built the great house, a showcase of wealth and power, between 1762 and 1764, to serve as the official residence for the Royal Governor. But it wasn't until elaborate remodeling–a new-framed coach house, stables, fencing, painting and wallpapering– by Royal Governor William Franklin had been completed, that the sole, illegitimate son of Benjamin Franklin took residence during October of 1774.

New Jersey was divided into East and West Jersey. The capital of East Jersey was Perth Amboy, while Burlington was the capital of West Jersey. Note how New Jersey's northern border extended into New York. There would be a series of skirmishes between the two colonies about the border between 1701 and 1765.

The seal of East Jersey.

In the short space of twelve years between 1763 and 1775, the ties that had bound Great Britain to her American colonies became strained to the breaking point. The residents of the colonies were torn between their sense of loyalty to the British Empire and their desire for liberty.

Together with his wife, Lady Elizabeth (Downes) Franklin, William Franklin resided here from 1774 to 1776. When relations between the Crown and the colonies deteriorated, his loyalty to King George III caused a tragic rift with his famous patriot father. While Benjamin chose to reject his mother country, his son chose to disobey his father. The elder Franklin never forgave his estranged son for his "disloyalty."

Our ghost hunter, Jane Doherty, could not resist commenting on my historical narrative: "Each soul has a path it walks and that is true of all of us; by our decisions we paint a portrait of who we really are."

At half-past three in the afternoon, we entered the mansion through its side door. Ready to begin her investigation, Jane exclaimed, "I definitely feel spirit presence here." It seemed to have touched her by its muteness, as if this mansion had become a tomb. (Jane was later to remark that her visit to the haunted

Proprietary House was the most fascinating case she had ever encountered.)

I led Jane into the colonial kitchen, with its massive fireplace and hard brick floor. "Why do I smell horses here?" she asked. Spirits, even animal ones, manifest themselves by smells and odors, I thought. "It was during the American Revolutionary War when the British soldiers would raid the city for livestock that patriots would stable their horses inside. And so it was, too, that this floor was used to stable horses," I replied. Horse ghosts were not exactly what we were expecting to discover!

The downstairs hall was especially active with spirit activity. "I sense children playing here," Jane said. It was as if she could hear the sound of little children's footsteps hallowing the past, silent voices calling her to commune with the consciousness of the souls of the deceased. "A long parade of children have lived and died in this place during the intervening years. Many others have reported sightings and children's voices in this hall," I replied.

Leading the way, I took Jane into the wine cellar, now used as a tearoom. Its inverted barrel-like ceiling of eighteenth century brick, fired in the kilns of Rahway, supported the heavy black-and-white marble floor that once existed above us, in the main floor reception hall. Admiring the bricks and stone of another age, Jane sensed spirits taking tea here. I shook my head in total amazement as I told Jane there have been several sightings of chairs pulled back from their normal places under tea tables. "It's as if some resting residents of this home for the dead rise to enjoy themselves here as the living do," Jane commented.

Across the long center hallway is the servants' hall, a lounge room where the many workers in this Palladian Georgian Palace would have spent some of their limited free time in the eighteenth century. There was a quiet and a chilly peace that infected the room, as if walking on a bridge from the present time to the past.

In a very real sense, the American Revolution was a civil war that turned family and friends against one another. The most famous example is how the conflict ended the relationship between Benjamin Franklin and his son, William. The younger Franklin served as New Jersey's last Royal Governor and remained a firm Loyalist. His portrait now hangs at the Proprietary House. The Proprietary House Association.

Is the shadowy feature
on the Proprietary
House steps a chemical
stain on photographer's
negative? Or is it the
spirit of one of the
departed souls said to
still inhabit the old
building?
Jack Dudas

The sound of thunder warned us of an approaching storm. We could not help noticing that the weather outside had rapidly changed. Soon we could hear the accompanying gusts of wind and the sound of rain pelting against the windows. Jane went on to explain that there is no such experience after death as we have constructed in our fear-based theologies. It is indeed possible to make a connection between two seemingly distant worlds. To perceive with unfrightened eyes through the nonchalance of death all that we simply do not see. "What a gift," I thought.

Jane then described how one could experience the unexpected. "Ghosts may touch you, stroke your hair, speak out loud or whisper in your ear, or brush against you as if you were walking through some cobwebs. Or you may hear footsteps or smell odors such as flowers, perfume, tobacco and alcohol associated with the deceased. They may manifest themselves in full body, dressed and looking just as real as you or I. The only difference is that when you approach them they will dissipate. However, spirits manifest themselves only when they want, and to whom they want. The more psychic energy present, the greater the potential for spiritual contact," she said. [It is in the Servants Hall here that the phenomena of glowing orbs as ancient as their representations in Egyptian tombs have been most recorded on camera.]

Did John Edward Prior, the celebrated Scottish architect and master builder of London, who designed this palatial manor house for the Proprietors of East Jersey, ever suspect that any of the forms of parapsychology, such as telepathy, clairvoyance, apparitions or any other supernatural phenomena might be experienced here? I wondered about the possibility. While these phenomena may seem incredible, and even unbelievable, it is all part of a day's work for ghost hunters and paranormal investigators like the amazing Jane Doherty.

The air was clearing, the sinister wind had subsided, and the fog was about to lift. Carefully we made our way up a narrow staircase through a low sloping corridor to reach the main floor. As if looking back through the ages, seeking glimpses of the great unseen, we entered the state dining room, shutting the door tightly.

Jane's sensitivity located spirit activity in two areas of the dining room. "The dimensions of this room are very regal," Jane commented as she slowly walked around its quiet corners. Soon she sensed the path of a female spirit. As Jane slowly followed this spirit's trail, it led her to the northeast window. "There is a woman who looks out of this window watching for someone," she said. Neighbors have sighted this woman, as have visiting Girl Scouts, I explained.

Moving again to her left, Jane stopped short and said, "Someone died right here–a man. Does that

Does the ghost of a little boy still knock on the imposing door of the Proprietary House?
The Proprietary House Association.

make any sense?" I drew a deep breath as Jane spoke. "Yes," I replied. "It was right where you are standing that a caretaker, Harold Reed, was found dead in the mid-1970s." I then showed Jane a photograph of a ghost taken entering the rear entrance to the building in 1976. We believe it was Harold Reed. Jane traced her finger across the sighting of this ghostly image as a chilly breeze passed us, leaving behind the odor of alcohol, like some silent dismembered form waiting to materialize. A trembling feeling suddenly filled my body. "Shall we move on now?" I uttered.

Entering the grand entrance hall, Jane paused by the heavy and imposing front door. It was as if she had been transported into a very intense daydream. I waited eagerly to learn what her next observation would be. "I sense a little boy knocking at this door," she said. Neighbors have reported ghostly sightings and unexplained noises, and have witnessed a little boy in blue who leaves a footprint-less path when he knocks on this very door with its iron knocker.

Jane continued into the hall and stopped short in the middle of the room, admiring the large restored portrait of William Franklin. I then related how his term in office began just as the colonial crises of the mid-eighteenth century were coming to a head. His judgments on Indian policy, creating the Lenni Lenape Reservation at Indian Mills in Burlington County, and his support for internal improvements and legal reforms, including chartering Rutgers University (then Queen's College) were well received in the colony. However, his unbending enforcement of the Stamp Act of November 1, 1765, traditionally identified as the start of the American Revolution, and hardline support for the government's policies, earned him the disdain of American patriots.

Jane then felt the presence of a young woman pacing through the grand entrance hall of the house, a hall that many accept as being haunted. I explained that some electricians had recently been working in

the mansion, and had noticed a woman dressed in a white gown standing here. Their voices quivered as they related their experience. When they approached her, she simply vanished into thin air. They all quit on the spot. I also felt a presence here, and noticed a dark form in my peripheral vision. As I turned with a sidelong glance to look straight at the dim image, it passed forward behind an arch, out of my line of vision. Up to this point I had been fascinated, but I had now been converted into a die-hard believer.

I was still trying to process all that we had seen and experienced in our brief foray into the past, when we rounded the corner to enter the Governor's housekeeper's room. What lurked in there was beyond belief. As we pushed the door ajar, as if bewitched by some voodoo charm from no earthly source, we heard an unseen spirit fling a heavy glass shelf from its secure moorings on a display cabinet into the center of the hardwood floor, shattering the glass into a thousand tiny pieces. Unconscious of what was going on about us, we had missed seeing the obvious—a surreal poltergeist phantom at play. Was this an eerie warning for us to leave? Even our ghost hunter, with her healthy level of skepticism, had to comment that something unexplainable was going on.

Jane, as if in a trance, now led the way into the

The Proprietary House as it appeared in the late 19th century.

Was it an angry spirit that sent a heavy glass shelf in the gift shop flying up and shattering on the floor? Circled is where the shelf *used* to be!

drawing room, seeking a rare glimpse of the governor whom the patriots deemed could no longer be trusted to govern. As we were soon to discover, like some ectoplasmic vapor hovering over this room, a William Franklin who refused to abandon his governor's residence was waiting there for us.

Drawn to the center of the room, Jane explained that it is here between the mantelpiece and the large Georgian wall mirror that William Franklin paces back and forth, frustrated and angry. Departing his solitude of death, this phantom man, long buried in England, has summoned himself here to relive his fateful decision to remain loyal to the Crown. Here he also relives glorious days of pomp and circumstance, as well as the dark periods of his life.

Prior to its major role in the American Revolution, New Jersey played a relatively minor part in the decade of protest that preceded the actual outbreak of war. By 1775 the colony-wide New Jersey Provincial Congress, and its Committee of Safety and Observation, had taken charge of the affairs of the colony in place of the increasingly isolated Royal Governor and his officials. It was in this charged political atmosphere that Benjamin Franklin, during a nine-day visit in September of 1775, made a visit here, strongly urging his son to join the rebel forces. William refused to acquiesce, and his decision initiated a

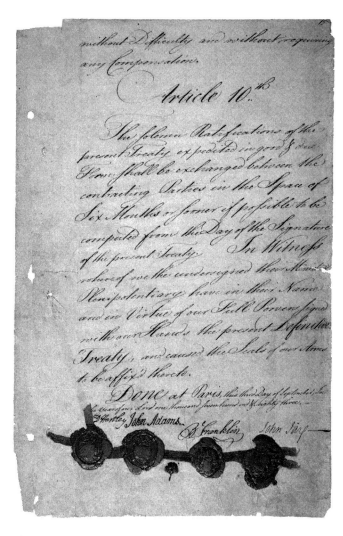

The signature page from the Treaty of Paris which officially ended the American Revolution on September 3, 1783. The third signature from the left is that of Benjamin Franklin. He never reconciled with his Loyalist son William Franklin.

lifelong rift between the two strong-willed men.

Tracking the past back to where it all began and unraveling the lengthening scroll of human fate, Jane felt the bitter and angry conversation taking place between William and his father. From two lives long since concluded, she felt the severe emotional pain of the Franklins, divided by a conflict that was as much a civil war as a war for independence; a war in which brothers fought brothers, fathers fought sons, and neighbors fought neighbors. The conflict split families, communities, and congregations, generating levels of

Quiens College ...

One of Governor William Franklin's lesser known legacies was his signing of the charter that founded Queens College, which later became Rutgers University.

hostility and brutality that changed lives irrevocably.

On June 19 1776, his Excellency, the Royal Governor, was arrested by the Middlesex County militia commanded by Col. Nathaniel Heard of Woodbridge. He was held in solitary confinement in Connecticut for 250 days, and was eventually set free during a prisoner exchange in November 1778. Upon his release, William fled to New York City and founded the Board of Associated Loyalists, while organizing resistance activities in Northern New Jersey and Long Island.

In August, 1782, with the war all but lost, Franklin fled into exile in England, hated by his fellow countrymen and disowned by the father he still venerated, and even loved. Lady Franklin remained at the Proprietary House for a short time, but eventually moved to British-controlled New York City. She died shortly thereafter without ever being reunited with her husband.

The ever-witty Benjamin Franklin had the final ironic word when William Franklin read the line in Benjamin's will which read: "The part he acted against me in the late war, which is of public notoriety, will account for my leaving him no more of an estate (than) he endeavored to deprive me of."

Like thousands of other Americans who had supported the losing side in America's first bloody civil war, William had lost his home, his personal property, and his rank in society, while also experiencing the pain of the loss of his beloved wife. He was destined to spend the next thirty years of his life in obscurity as a lonely exile in England, never fully accepted by a British government that turned down the majority of his claims for financial loss. When he died on November 13, 1813, he could finally rest in peace—or could he?

Macabre as it may seem, like some silent dismembered form waiting to materialize as a chilly breeze out of a long closed vault, William Franklin has returned to his Proprietary House. His ghostly image seems to infect the Grand Parlor with its psychic energy. Quietly he leaves a footprint-less path as he treads those same steps of his luminous and vibrant past. Departing his solitude of death, frustrated and angry, his earthly remains no longer existent, this bodiless phantom man, like some ectoplasmic vapor, summons himself here. You may feel his ghostly chill, and if you listen closely, you may even hear him moan.

When William Franklin died in 1813, he was buried at St. Pancras Church in London. This image is believed to show the old church as it existed in 1815. Does his spirit still rest there? Or does he haunt the Proprietary House, reliving his decision to remain loyal to the Crown?

These astonishing experiences that I engaged in with Jane Doherty at the Proprietary House persuaded me that psychic phenomena are a normal part of life. Those who seem to be resting do rise on occasion! As we left the complex, pondering the mysterious world of the past that Jane had helped to unravel, life here suddenly seemed so very sweet. It felt so good to be alive! Although still commanding our attention, the long parade of New Jersey's Royal Governors has ended, but the Proprietary House, the monument to their rule, endures as it has for centuries.

Saving the Historic Indian Queen Tavern

East Jersey Olde Town, Piscataway, NJ

*R*egretfully, almost all signs of colonial New Brunswick have now vanished. Commander-in-Chief George Washington visited here at periods of both defeat and victory. Highways and corporate complexes now cover what were once exceptionally important historical sites. Occupied for a time by the British, most major British generals spent time here, including Commander-in-Chief General Sir William Howe. In fact, a direct attempt was made on his life on March 9, 1777, while he was in New Brunswick.

In 1759, as a heroic young lieutenant colonel during the French and Indian War, William Howe had led a detachment of light infantry up the steep embankments of Quebec, thus making way for the army of Major General James Wolfe during their defeat of the French under Montcalm on the Plains of Abraham. In the Battle of Bunker Hill, in June 1775, when the British suffered 1,000 casualties before gaining that high ground, Howe had marched in the front line, quickly learning not to underestimate the enemy.

Nothing is left of White Hall Tavern (built circa 1756) where Washington lodged while en route to take command of the Continental Army.

Washington also celebrated July 4, 1778 there after his strategic victory at the Battle of Monmouth. The subsequent court-martial, in part, of General Charles Lee for insubordination also took place there.

Like White Hall Tavern, Peter Cochrane's rambling tavern witnessed a great deal of activity during the war. It too, no longer exists. It served as headquarters for Washington from November 29 until December 1, 1776, during the "Long Retreat" across New Jersey. It was also one of the hiding places, in 1779, of Lieutenant Colonel John Graves Simcoe, credited as being one of the finest and cleverest field commanders in the British Army. It was he who was notorious for his burning and looting of the Raritan Valley.

The Buccleuch Mansion, built in 1739, was home to Anthony White. It still stands in Buccleuch Park.
Image by "Baronplantagenet," Wikipedia.org

The Neilson House, headquarters for Sir William Howe from December 2, 1776 to June 22, 1777, was torn down in the 1870s. It was Colonel John Neilson who had first read the Declaration of Independence to the citizens of New Brunswick on the town green on July 9, 1776. Summoned to the reading by the only bell in New Brunswick, located in the stone tower of Christ Church, the people of the city listened intently to one of the first recitations of the document in the new nation.

Still standing is the Buccleuch Mansion, a gracious Georgian Mansion built in 1739, and now the focal point of the picturesque 78-acre Buccleuch Park. This estate residence in New Brunswick was originally known as the White House Farm, after its first owner, Anthony White.

White was a friend of George Washington, and entertained him for a time as guest of honor here. Washington was said to have favorably compared the house and grounds to his own estate. He later visited

(Previous page)
Sir William Howe from a color mezzotint dated November 1777 by Richard Purcell, aka Charles Corbutt (c.1736-c.1766).

Among the luminaries of the American Revolution who stayed at the Indian Queen Tavern was George Washington (top) and John Adams. This portrait of Washington, by Charles Willson Peale in 1772, is the earliest known, showing him in uniform as colonel of the Virginia Regiment. The portrait of John Adams, by Gilbert Stuart, shows him later in life, as the second U.S. President.

the house as a guest of Colonel Charles Stewart.

White married Elizabeth Morris, daughter of Royal Governor Lewis Morris, who was also a leading Proprietor and Chancellor. The house was purchased in 1774 by British General William Burton, and during the Revolutionary War it housed British soldiers on several occasions when the British occupied New Brunswick (December 1776 to June 1777). At that time, the Enniskillen Guards (from present-day Northern Ireland) occupied the third floor.

Since 1914, the Jersey Blue Chapter of the National Society Daughters of the American Revolution, (NSDAR, founded in 1890), has assumed the care of the interior and furnishings of the 16-room Buccleuch mansion, and interprets it significance under the mantel of their motto "God, Home, and Country."

The Indian Queen Tavern formerly stood for 241 years at the northwest corner of Albany and Water Streets in the center of New Brunswick. Reported to have been built in 1729 as a one-story home, it was expanded to two stories and later operated as the Bell Tavern or Bell Hotel. It underwent countless renovations, the most lasting being of the late Georgian period, when a third floor was added. As with many eighteenth century buildings, the supporting walls of the building were unnecessarily overbuilt. The original walls were about two feet thick, which was not essential for support or insulation, since the tavern originally contained two massive central chimneys with sixteen flues apiece.

At the peak of its popularity during the American Revolution, George Washington, John Adams and other colonial public officials were among its many guests. It served as a place where prominent Revolutionary War figures dined and rested from their travels. It was also a well-known setting for government meetings, and a place to take in the news of the outside world. Plain outspoken talk of civil war turned its smoky taproom gray.

After my long involvement with the Proprietary House in Perth Amboy, NJ and before that with the restoration of the Montrose School House in Colts Neck, NJ, I had identified with the story of how the Indian Queen was saved. It takes the dedication of one key person, along with committed individuals, all working in concert, to make it happen. Jane could relate to my passion, and had come to the Indian Queen to see it for herself. As I described tavern life in the eighteenth century, Jane had the distinct sense that "treason was brewing and revolution was in the air!"

I explained to Jane that taverns or inns were an absolute necessity during colonial times. In fact, a 1668 law ordered every East Jersey town to provide an "ordinary" for the relief and entertainment of strangers. The local "ordinary" was a social and political center of unrivaled importance. Public meetings, balls, elections and celebrations were regularly held there. The taproom was constantly enlivened by the presence of local gentry assembled for gossip and frivolity.

The tavern was the social center of the community, where major affairs took place, where revolution was fomented, and where local news was exchanged. Visitors and townspeople all gathered in a main assembly room in front of a fireplace. After drinks were dispensed and food served, guests raised

Taverns, inns and ale-houses were an integral part of colonial life in America, transported from the public house traditions of England. They were a center of civic life as well as a pleasant place to quench one's thirst. This painting, "The Ale-House Door" was painted by Henry Singleton in 1790.

Thanks to the hard work of Dr. Joseph Kler, the Indian Queen Tavern was rescued and removed with other colonial era buildings to the East Jersey Olde Towne village he founded in 1974.

their voices in a roaring song or in a heated argument. Probably no other institution played such a lively and vital role in colonial society. Sleeping rooms were commonly situated above the taproom, and guests often slept two or more to a bed.

An act passed by the New Jersey Legislature in 1679 absolutely forbade the sale of any intoxicating liquors whatsoever to Indians. Intoxicated Indians were to be seized and kept in confinement until they named the person from whom they had obtained the liquor. By 1682, licensed tavern-keepers and tapsters were held accountable in a measure for the excesses of their guests. "Interesting, this is not a new idea." Jane said.

A 1704 New Jersey law sentenced four hours in the stocks for public drunkenness, and forbade anyone to "tipple and drink on the Lord's Day," a stricture considerably watered down by the clause "excepting for necessary refreshments."

A law against selling liquors to servants and slaves, without the permission of their masters, was reenacted in 1751. In 1758, an act "for building barracks within the colony" provided that any tavern-keeper who sold liquor to common soldiers, without permission of their commanding officers, or from a justice of the peace, should forfeit forty shillings.

In 1768, the New Jersey Provincial Assembly passed an act making it the duty of the court to ascertain, before issuing any license, whether the tavern-keeper applicant possessed sufficient means to enable him to provide a certain number of featherbeds for the use of travelers, as well as stabling and pasturage for horses.

I explained to Jane that the Indian Queen Tavern was threatened with demolition as part of the expansion of Route 18 in 1971. Joseph Henry Kler, M.D., F.A.C.S., humanitarian, community leader, philanthropist, and local historian, who had devoted his professional and personal life to the people of Central New Jersey, was the first to speak out against the destruction of this historic property, and to take the initiative to preserve it.

Dr. Kler quickly assembled a group of friends, raised funds, and negotiated the removal of the Indian Queen Tavern from its original site. As a result, the structure became the first piece in a mosaic that would preserve the visual record of New Jersey culture, known as East Jersey Olde Towne (originally a non-profit organization that Dr. Kler founded in 1974).

Both Dr. Kler and his wife, Elizabeth Van Hosen Vaughn, had a sincere love for American history. During the 1960s, Mrs. Kler served as Curator for the Daughters of the American Revolution, and assumed the same role at Buccleuch Mansion, in Buccleuch Park. She also chaired the Christmas Ball at the mansion for many years.

After the death of her father on November 21, 1983, Marjorie V. Kler Freeman, the couple's daughter, who had worked alongside her father since the inception of East Jersey Olde Towne, both as curator and director, was elected President of East Jersey Olde Towne, Inc.

Major General John Sullivan and Brigadier General James Clinton led an expedition in 1779 against Loyalists and their allies, the Four Nations Confederation formed by the Iroqois. Following only one battle with the British at Newton, New York, (which they handily won) they returned to New Jersey, while systematically burning some forty Iroqois villages along the way. The devastation ended Iroqois attacks on American settlements but also left thousands of refugees, many of who froze to death. This monument at Lodi, New York commemorates the expedition.

In May 1989, East Jersey Olde Towne, Inc. gifted the buildings to the people of Middlesex County. The Middlesex County Cultural and Heritage Commission now administers this nationally acclaimed historic site, known today as East Jersey Olde Towne village.

Nationally acclaimed historic site East Jersey Olde Towne village, adjacent to Johnson Park (the county's second largest park), is near the "River Road Historic District" of Piscataway. It is on one of the earliest New Jersey transportation corridors, which had its origin as a Native American footpath used in summer to travel to the coast. The homes that line this historic road are vernacular adaptations of a variety of styles, including Dutch Colonial, Federal, Greek revival and Victorian.

Located on twelve acres, the village grew into a living history interpretation of the culture and everyday life of the early settlers of Central New Jersey. The Indian Queen Tavern was reconstructed here, from a mixture of new and original materials, between 1976 and 1980. In 2006, it was professionally restored and re-opened to the public. It houses a fascinating exhibit that interprets its own history, as well as that of other similar establishments in Central New Jersey. The story of the endless restoration effort by the few, and the tireless preservation dedication of the many, impressed Jane greatly.

Eager to learn more, I then told Jane that one of the most intriguing tales of the Indian Queen Tavern began on Saturday, August 31, 1776, when George Washington informed the Continental Congress that "General Sullivan says [British Admiral] Lord [Richard] Howe is extremely desirous of seeing some of the members of Congress . . ." (Lord Howe in fact did suggest a meeting with delegates of the Continental Congress on New York's

Staten Island).

During the Battle of Long Island on August 27, the British had succeeded in capturing General John Sullivan, the commander of the defeated American forces. As an officer, Sullivan had been treated well, and had dined and conversed with Admiral Howe, who persuaded him to help arrange a face-to-face meeting with members of Congress. Admiral Howe released Sullivan on parole as an emissary to Congress. Arriving in Philadelphia on September 2, Sullivan appeared before Congress on September 3 to deliver Lord Howe's request for a "Peace Conference." Taking the floor in protest, the patriot who was to become the second President of the United States, John Adams, called Sullivan "a decoy duck whom Lord Howe has sent among us to seduce us into a renunciation of our independence."

Benjamin Franklin (top), John Adams (left) and Edward Rutledge (below) were sent by George Washington to meet with Lord Howe for an abortive peace conference on Staten Island.

While Sullivan was addressing Congress, Adams muttered under his breath to Dr. Benjamin Rush, who was sitting beside him, that he wished the first shot fired by the British in the Long Island battle had gone through Sullivan's head. After four days of debate, it was decided that a committee of Peace Commissioners consisting of John Adams, Benjamin Franklin and Edward Rutledge be sent to meet with Lord Howe.

On September 8 Benjamin Franklin wrote to George Washington, "The Congress having appointed Mr.

Adams, Mr. Rutledge and myself to meet Lord Howe and hear what Propositions he may have to make, we purpose setting out to-morrow and to be at Perth Amboy on Wednesday morning . . . What we have heard of the Badness of the Roads between that Place and New York makes us wish to be spar'd that part of the Journey."

On Monday, September 9, the three Peace Commissioners set out from Philadelphia. Accompanied by a servant, Franklin and Rutledge each rode in a high, two-wheeled chaise. Adams rode on horseback and was accompanied by Joseph Bass, his frequent traveling companion.

The road across New Jersey was filled with soldiers marching to join Washington, mostly Pennsylvania men. As a consequence, with the roads crowded and dusty, the journey took two days. Upon their arrival in New Brunswick, the Indian Queen Tavern was so full that Adams and Franklin had to share the same bed in a tiny room with only one small window. Franklin, as one of seventeen children, had no complaint with this arrangement. However, Adams would describe the situation differently:

"The first night we lodged at an Inn in Brunswick . . . The Taverns were so full we could with difficulty obtain Entertainment. At Brunswick, but one bed could be procured for Dr. Franklin and me in a chamber little larger than the bed, without a Chimney, and with only one small Window. The Window was open, and I, who was an invalid and afraid of the Air in the night, shut it close. 'Oh!' says Franklin, 'don't shut the window. We shall be suffocated.' I answered I was afraid of the Evening Air. Dr. Franklin replied, 'the Air within this Chamber will soon be, and indeed now is, worse than that without Doors. Come, open the Window and come to bed, and I will convince you. I believe you are not acquainted with my Theory of Colds.' Opening the Window, and leaping into Bed, I said I had read his Letters to Dr. Cooper, in which he had advanced that Nobody ever got cold by going into a cold Church or any other cold air; but the Theory was so little consistent with my experience that I thought it a Paradox...The Doctor then began an harangue upon Air and Cold and Respiration and Perspiration, with which I was so much amused that I soon fell asleep and left him and his philosophy together..."

On Wednesday, September 11, 1776, the American Peace Commissioners left New Brunswick and continued to Perth Amboy. There they crossed the Arthur Kill on Lord Howe's opulent red-and-gilt barge for a meeting–an abortive peace conference. Lord Howe had made it abundantly clear, wrote his Secretary Henry Strachey, that he could not confer with them as members of Congress–that he "could not acknowledge that body which was not acknowledged by the king, whose delegate he was"–and that therefore could only consider them "merely as gentlemen of great ability and influence," i.e., as private persons.

Adams was quick with his reply: "Your Lordship may consider me in what light you please, and indeed, I should be willing to consider myself, for a few moments, in any character which would be agreeable to your Lordship, except that of a British subject."

Howe then turned to Franklin and Rutledge and remarked, "Mr. Adams is a decided character." A few years later, Adams would better comprehend the gloomy look on Howe's face. Before leaving London, Adams learned that Howe had been given a list of those American rebels who were to be granted pardons and those who were not. John Adams was one of the latter, and his penalty would have been death by hanging.

The Conference House

Home of Christopher Billopp

One of colonial New York's most unusual residences is Captain Christopher Billopp's magnificent grand stone house, "the Manor of Bentley," built circa 1685. It is markedly different, both in style and scale, from the scattered Dutch and English farmhouses typically found on Staten Island. Built by Scottish stonemasons from Perth Amboy, this ancient-looking fieldstone residence, impressively bold in appearance, is characteristic of the Medieval influence on some early colonial architecture. In keeping with his role as a leading member of New York's provincial government and as an expression of his massive wealth, it stood as an important symbol of the stability of the colonies. Now restored, it is filled with eighteenth century furniture and exhibitions of life in colonial times, and is open to visitors.

On a slight rise looking out over Raritan Bay, this National and New York City landmark is the lone survivor of seventeenth century buildings still standing in New York City, and the only surviving monument to the manor life of that time period. This tidewater residence is the centerpiece of the 226-acre Conference House Park, located in the southernmost tip of Tottenville. It serves as a fine reminder of Staten Island's rural and maritime past, as well as the borough's place in American history. Archaeological evidence suggests that Native Americans not only had a village on this site, but are probably buried here.

Surrounded by a diverse forest ecosystem, which is a natural stopover for migrating birds, the park's coastline is a suitable place to enjoy spectacular marine views of open sky, cloud formations, the Great Beds Lighthouse and the sunset. The park is a short distance from the Mount Loretto State Nature

Preserve, featuring stunning vistas of Raritan Bay from natural red clay cliff bluffs. The dark sandy shore of the preserve gives way to cobblestone-sized glacial rocks, as well as giant-sized boulders at the water's edge. The beach is dotted with broken oyster shells, soft shell clams buried in the sand, and bits of surf-smoothed green beach grass.

On the date that Jane and I visited the house, June 21ˢᵗ, it was a warm summer's evening. Fast-moving clouds were passing quickly around the setting sun. The wind was signing softly and the waters of the bay seemed to be edging closer with the rising of the tide. Looking out onto this watery highway of the seventeenth century, we stood quietly, absorbing the scene around us. "What a lovely place to get in touch with the things of the soul," Jane said softly.

Drawing a clue from the surroundings, she then explained that we have harmed ourselves greatly by not cultivating the art of not doing. "First we lost the gift of the quiet mind, open to intuition and insight. Then we forced our wills and our reason into every situation and lost our creativity along the way. We need to relearn the wisdom of the old cliché that says 'don't just do something, sit there'."

The time had come to step into the dim corridors of the past. Turning away from the bay, we now headed towards the Conference House to see things that were once seen, but can be observed no more. In the fading twilight, the grand illumination of candlelight that glowed from the same windows of the house that let

The Manhattan skyline had humble beginnings. This sketch, possibly by artist Thomas Davies in the 1770s, is thought to have been made from Long Island and shows the Rutgers House in the foreground. New York City is the small collection of buildings on the horizon. The steeple is that of Trinity Church. The Conference House on Staten Island is the sole survivor of these 18th century vistas.

in both the sun and sea air illuminated our path up the great south lawn to the manor house itself.

Mesmerized, we entered through the substantial wooden front door into what was, by all appearances, the eighteenth century world. Our guide first invited us to visit the basement level, which ultimately turned out to be the eeriest part of the tour. This level contains the original large shadowy kitchen, complete with its massive fireplace and baking oven, its ceiling held up by hand-hewn beams. Jane sensed the tread of backward and forward footsteps, no doubt some disembodied listener walking back and forth across the room.

Turning to the right, we entered a large vaulted root cellar, like some undiscovered Egyptian tomb, filled with psychic energy. Jane deduced that there was a tunnel beneath this floor, about fifteen feet or so below the surface, and that it led to the waterfront. "It's large enough for a horse and carriage," she ventured. Our guide confirmed that there is a legend about a tunnel's existence, but none has ever been found.

Ascending the staircase, we then proceeded to a second floor bedchamber. Here Jane sensed an older girl's spirit, once lodged in the warmth of her body, still caring for her two younger sisters. "Things are definitely not what they seem to be," I thought. For here in this children's room these girls, like angels at play, dissolve like the darkness into dawn.

The Billopp House as it appeared in a 19th century engraving that was published in *Appletons Encyclopedia*.

At the top of the staircase was a small room once used as a study. Starring out of the window, Jane let out a heavy yet almost inaudible sigh. "I sense a man standing here watching troops across the bay through his spy glass." Colonel   Christopher

Billopp was known to have done this. I explained that he commanded a corps of Loyalist militia and was a member of the Provincial government. He had agreed that his ancestral family home be used for the sole meeting of the British and Colonials, with the expectation of removing political obstacles in the way of a return of the colonies to their allegiance to the king.

After the Revolution, his property of more than 1,600 acres, including Billopp House, was confiscated by the insipient State of New York. Like so many Loyalists, he emigrated to Nova Scotia and later settled in New Brunswick, Canada, where his family was given land by the king of England as a token for their loyalty to the Crown.

Returning to the main floor, we entered the Billopp family parlor, which, like the other rooms, was beautifully restored and tastefully furnished with eighteenth century pieces. Jane walked quietly around the perimeter of the room, as if stepping in the same luminous footprints of those who were part of the vibrant past here. As if looking backward across the centuries, seeking glimpses of the great unseen, Jane explained that a conference of great historical significance had taken place here. She specifically mentioned Benjamin Franklin and John Adams, and sensed that there were other participants present as well.

Then, like a gust of chill, damp wind out of a long-closed vault, Jane felt the presence of Colonel Christopher Billopp. I shall never forget the expression on her face when she said, "He wants the world to know that he, too, was present for that historic conference." I explained that Lord Howe's Secretary, Henry Strachey, recorded all that took place at the conference, but did not include mention of Colonel Christopher Billopp as being present. Having no prior knowledge of Billopp House or the historic conference, Jane asked me to describe the facts that

Frederick North, 2nd Earl of Guilford, served as Great Britain's Prime Minister from 1770 to 1782. He assigned Lord Howe to offer the colonies a peace agreement, but American ambitions for independence had grown too strong to go back. He resigned in 1782 after a motion of no confidence from his government following the British defeat at Yorktown the year before.

not even her intuition could have discerned.

With the Declaration of Independence adopted by Congress on July 4, 1776, war had officially begun. But while the Declaration made clear the issues of individual liberties and freedoms from the king of Great Britain, colonists still had to decide which was more important–their desire for independence or their loyalty to the mother country.

It had been Admiral Lord Richard Howe's sincere hope that peace with the Americans could be achieved. Commander of His Majesty's Atlantic Squadron and Member of Parliament, British Prime Minister Lord North later appointed him Acting Peace Commissioner. As early as January 1776, Lord North had charged Lord Howe to lead a peace commission. American allegiances at this time were divided. Lord Howe knew very well that about one third of the colonists were supporters of independence, while Loyalists made up another third of the colonial population. The last third remained neutral for the time being, waiting to see what the future would bring.

By June 29, 1776, more than 100 of Lord Howe's transports, which sailed from Halifax, Nova Scotia, had dropped anchor off Sandy Hook. As late as June 30 the great Province of New York would not release its delegates to the Continental Congress to vote for independence. Arriving eight days after the Declaration was signed, Lord Howe, on July 12, 1776, landed 15,000 troops on Staten Island to add to the forces already under command of his brother General William Howe.

On July 13, General Howe sent out letters to the colonial governors written by Admiral Howe, explaining his peace initiative. A lieutenant carried them from Staten Island to Perth Amboy, where he distributed them to American couriers. This despite the advice the Admiral had given to his brother that they would have little impact now that the Declaration of

Independence had been signed. By mid-August, a total of some 35,000 British troops, the largest British expeditionary force ever sent overseas prior to the great embarkations and landings of World War I and II, were stationed on Staten Island.

John Trumbull painted this heroic representation of the Battle of Princeton, showing George Washington on horseback and a British soldier bayonetting Brigadier General Hugh Mercer. Washington put Mercer in charge of his "Flying Camp" at Perth Amboy in June of 1776.

The spectacle of thousands of disciplined Redcoats drilling on a parade ground, with only the Arthur Kill separating them from Perth Amboy, created panic. By June 1776, Washington had hastily organized a "Flying Camp" at Perth Amboy under Brigadier General Hugh Mercer. It consisted of New Jersey, Pennsylvania, Delaware, and Maryland militia, a total of about 1,200 men, all poised to repel any British advance into New Jersey. The Perth Amboy patriots used the steeple of St. Peter's Church (the oldest Anglican parish in New Jersey, founded in 1698) as a watchtower to monitor British and Tory activity across the Arthur Kill and on Staten Island. Their highly mobile attack units were also positioned at Bergen Point, Bergen Neck, and Paulus Hook, from where they could be quickly deployed if fighting broke out. Shortly after the arrest of Royal Governor William Franklin on June 19, 1776, General Mercer made the Proprietary House at Amboy

The top of Captain William Bryant's gravestone (above) is said to have been shot off by a round from a British frigate firing at an American cannon set up in the churchyard. The hole in Gertrude Hay's marker (below) was believed to have been the result of the same engagement.

his headquarters.

General Mercer encountered countless frustrations as he sought to organize his command. Militia companies arrived and departed almost daily, with the result that no orderly troop disposition could be made. As the weeks dragged on without the anticipated attack, the men became restless and clamored to return to their homes. By July 20, most of the New Jersey troops, the majority of whom where farmers, had been temporarily excused to harvest hay in their sun-baked fields.

Lord Howe was the head of a powerful aristocratic family. Navy men affectionately called him "Black Dick" because of his dark skin and the fearlessness he had displayed under fire while chasing French ships during the Seven Years' War. More ominous than his brother William, he held off invading Perth Amboy, as his goal was to secure New York City and possibly make peace.

Early in the war, some Flying Camp militiamen from Woodbridge planted an eighteen pounder (cannon) between breastworks in St. Peter's Churchyard and opened fire on a British man-of-war ship. The British frigate's return gunfire broke the gravestone of Captain William Bryant, a fragment of which can still be seen in the churchyard. Bryant's daughter, Mary, married William Peartree Smith, an ardent patriot, member of the Committee of Safety and Observation and a trustee of the College of New Jersey. The gravestone of Gertrude Hay (d. 1733) has a hole in it supposedly made during the same encounter.

Here at historic old St. Peter's Church, during a less stressful time, Royal Governor William Franklin and his wife were provided with a private pew, as was the custom of those times. They presented hand embroidered linen and hangings for the pulpit, and a reading desk and altar, complete with matching cushions made by Lady Franklin. Here they received Holy Communion from the hand-wrought chalice and paten cover of communion silver which the church had received as a gift from Queen Anne in about 1706. (It is marked "Annae Reginae," and was crafted by William Gibson, Corey Lane, London, who first registered his maker's mark in April 1697).

On August 22, 1776, the Howes landed 15,000 British troops near the Narrows of Long Island, in a decisive move to impress upon George Washington and his Continental Army the need to negotiate a peaceful settlement. The British army and the American rebels subsequently engaged at the Battle of Long Island on August 27 (the first great battle of the war and a colossal defeat for the Continental Army), resulting in Washington's withdrawing of his army of 9,500 men to Manhattan.

The Battle of Long Island–later called the Battle of Brooklyn, as the majority of the action took place across the entire area of today's Borough of Brooklyn–had been the largest battle ever fought in North America. Counting both armies and the Royal Navy, more than 40,000 men had taken part in it.

Not eager to draw further American bloodshed, Lord Howe sheathed his sword and held out the olive

Queen Anne as she appeared in a 1702 painting by John Closterman, four years before sending Perth Amboy's St. Peter's church a handwrought chalice.

General George Washington personally orchestrated the successful retreat of the Continental Army during the Battle of Long Island as celebrated by an engraving by J.C. Armytage from painting by M.A. Wageman.

branch of peace. The king had given him authority to issue pardons to all rebels who would remain "in peaceable obedience" to the king.

By September 5, the new American Congress assented to a peace conference, not expecting Lord Howe to bend, but curious to know more about his intentions. Representative Benjamin Franklin represented the Middle Colonies, with John Adams acting as the delegate from New England, and Edward Rutledge standing in for the South.

On September 8, Franklin suggested that the conference take place "either at the house on Staten Island opposite Amboy, or at the governor's house in Amboy." Admiral Howe had already requisitioned the Billopp House and estate for the enormous British army billeted on Staten Island, with troops tented on the property surrounding the manor house. Howe chose the Billopp House, where their meeting would later be both evoked and enshrined. It was the site of the only face-to-face meeting between the British and the Americans during the entire war.

Howe chose the intimidating Grenadiers to stand as guards between which the American delegates had to pass. The Grenadiers shown here wear their distinctive mitre helmets, though these would have been replaced by bearskin helmets when the meeting took place.

As previously mentioned, the American Peace Commissioners departed Philadelphia on September 9, staying at the Indian Queen Tavern in New Brunswick, before arriving at Perth Amboy on September 11. As arranged, the Americans met Lord Howe's red-and-gilt barge at the foot of Smith Street in Perth Amboy. After crossing the Arthur Kill, they were escorted up the great south lawn of Billopp House by Lord Howe, between lines of guards of grenadiers "looking as fierce as the ten Furies," Adams later recalled.

Adams took careful note of Howe's hospitality: "The house had been the

habitation of military guards and was as dirty as a stable; but his Lordship had prepared a large handsome room by spreading a carpet of moss and green sprigs from bushes and shrubs in the neighborhood, till he made it not only wholesome, but romantically elegant, and he entertained us with good claret, good bread, cold hams, tongues and mutton." Following a half-hour lunch, the table was cleared and the conference began.

The Conference House still stands on Staten Island as the centerpiece of Conference House Park overlooking Raritan Bay.

I mentioned to Jane, "Lord Howe must have thought, 'What are these traitors thinking about? Do they really think that they can succeed against the strength of the world's most powerful nation?' And in the minds of the Americans there must have been the thought 'perhaps the American experiences described in the Declaration of Independence that governments are instituted among men, deriving their just powers

Nathan Hale was
honored on a half cent
U.S. Postage stamp
issued in 1925 and 1929.
The portrait was based
on a statue by Bela Lyon
Pratt erected at the
Chicago Tribune Tower.
He was hanged as an
American spy near
Beekman House in
Manhattan, which had
been used by General
Howe as his
headquarters.

James Beekman's
ancestors summered in
this Perth Amboy house
between 1884 and 1928.

from the consent of the governed and that they have the power to absolve themselves from all allegiance to the British Crown was foreign to the Howes.' Howe's failure to recognize American independence was the immediate cause of the breakdown of their meeting long after referred to as the "Abortive Peace Conference."

On September 12, Washington's war council decided to abandon New York City. By September 15, the British had landed at Kip's Bay and routed a small resident force of American militia. The American army fled to Harlem as the British re-occupied New York City, which then became the British military headquarters in America.

General Howe established his headquarters at Mount Pleasant, one of Manhattan's most splendid estates. Owned by James Beekman and overlooking the East River, this house stood near today's First Avenue and Fifty-first Street. (Incidentally, between 1884 and 1928, Beekman family members "summered" at their home in Perth Amboy at 1 Lewis Street). Howe may have chosen the Beekman mansion for its beauty, but its strategic location also had military advantages: It placed Howe in the center of his command, midway between the city and the main body of the army to the north, and not far from the brigade he had left behind to secure Long Island.

I shared with Jane that it was later, at the greenhouse attached to Beekman House, that Nathan Hale, the patriot spy, was kept prisoner the night before he was hanged (an incident which took place near present day Third Avenue and Sixty-sixth Street). Hale would long be remembered for his famous last words, "I only regret that I have but one life to lose for my country."

The importance of defending New York City for the

Americans had been based more on Washington's political judgment than on his military strategy. He had bitterly learned this lesson from the devastating loss of American lives when the British overtook Fort Washington. This was a lesson that was to soon serve him well in New Jersey.

On October 12, the British landed 4,000 men on Throg's Neck, but were soon stopped by American riflemen. Then on October 18, Washington withdrew his main army to White Plains while Howe withdrew his forces from Throg's Neck and made a swift landing at Pell's Point, engaging the Americans in the Battle of White Plains on October 28.

Sir Henry Clinton replaced General Howe Howe in the Spring of 1778, after British losses at the Battles of Trenton and Princeton. This painting is believed to have been created by Italian artist Andrea Soldi sometime between 1762 and 1765.

From there Washington's forces shifted to North Castle, crossing the Hudson River at King's Ferry on November 12, and arriving in Haverstraw, New York. They moved on to Fort Lee, New Jersey the next day. Lacking American sea power, the simple truth was that New York had been indefensible. John Adams' description of New York as "a kind of key to the whole continent" had been right on the mark.

Unanticipated at the peace conference between Howe and the Americans on September 11, 1776, two brilliant victories against the British troops would take place on Christmas night, 1776–one at Trenton, and another eight days later at Princeton. By the spring of 1778, a new Commander-in-Chief of the British forces in America, Sir Henry Clinton had replaced the Howes. It wouldn't be until the signing of the Treaty of Paris in 1783 (largely drafted by Benjamin Franklin) that His Britannic Majesty, King George III, would acknowledge the thirteen colonies "to be free, sovereign, and independent states."

As we approached the heavy front entrance door of the Conference House once again, the tall case clock in the hall struck midnight. Looking out at the dark bay, the scene gave the impression that the stars had all been extinguished like candles. It had been a fascinating visit, and we graciously thanked our guide.

Where had the time gone on this solstice, the longest day of the year?

We made our way carefully down to the water's edge, watching the full moon rise. Jane stared with me across the water as we watched the moonlight shimmer on beautiful Raritan Bay. The lunar force has its strongest effect on the tides at full moon, I thought. "Moonlight," said Jane "This is my kind of time!" Across the Arthur Kill Sound, we could see the glimmering city lights of Perth Amboy.

Hindsight offers us what no one moment in the present is capable of doing. Looking backward again, across the ages, I thought how unavoidably we are all connected to the past. The shoreline hadn't changed; it was just as it was when the three great American patriots arrived here on September 11, 1776.

We continued to stand quietly on that warm windless night, listening to gentle waves lapping against the shore. With thoughts of both the Loyalists and patriots still vividly in mind, I could not help thinking of all the sights these shores had witnessed during the past four hundred years.

As a last pleasure to cap off what had been a perfect day, we witnessed horseshoe crabs emerge from Raritan Bay onto the beach, as they do every May and June during full moon. These prehistoric creatures, which have existed for more than 1.2 billion years, resemble a crab in appearance, but are actually more closely related to the spider and the scorpion. "They have come to lay their eggs. One female can lay up to 20,000 tiny olive-green eggs in a hole in the sand which she carefully prepares," I said. "How fortunate for us to witness such a sight," Jane replied. "How fascinating to think that the vision of liberty and freedom embodied in the Declaration of Independence and the life that comes from the sea continue to survive just as they have for all these years."

Part Two

Defeat, Retreat &
Victory

New Jersey's Darkest Hour

Our narrative begins with the Stocktons, Princeton's most legendary American Revolutionary family. Historic Morven, an imposing Georgian house in the center of Princeton, was the home of Richard Stockton III, signer of the Declaration of Independence, and his wife, Annis Boudinot Stockton, who named the house after a mythical Gaelic kingdom. It stands on land purchased in October 1701 by his great-grandfather, Richard Stockton, called "The Settler," or "First Immigrant," from William Penn, a Proprietor of West Jersey. The west wing, the earliest surviving section of the house, was built in 1758. Five successive generations of the Stockton family lived here. This New Jersey historic treasure has recently been restored and opened to the public. I was eager for Jane to see it. Keenly interested, Jane pressed me for more details.

In those days, when Princeton was a small village, a constant stream of travelers passed by Morven, which was conveniently situated on the King's Highway, which ran from Elizabeth Point across the Raritan River at (New Brunswick) to the Falls of the Delaware at Trenton. This main thoroughfare of Princeton, now called Nassau Street, is believed to have followed the original Native American trail between the Raritan and Delaware Rivers. Princeton was named "Prince-Town" in honor of Prince William of Orange and Nassau.

Annis Boudinot Stockton was the sister of Elias Boudinot IV, President of the Continental Congress, who resided at Morven during their Princeton session in 1783. Between June and November of that year, Princeton Borough was the *de facto* national Capital. The Continental Congress,

Richard Stockton

threatened by unpaid soldiers in Philadelphia, moved its deliberations to Nassau Hall on Nassau Street. It was during that session that Congress thanked Washington in person for his achievements during the war. Elias Boudinot had also served as President when the Continental Congress ratified the Treaty of Paris, making peace with Great Britain, and thus ending the war.

Sparked with interest about Annis and Richard Stockton, Jane wanted to know more about them. I explained that Annis was an ardent patriot, poet, and friend of George Washington. Elias Boudinot and others regularly saw to it that her poems to George Washington were placed in print. Her poem "Addressed to General George Washington, in 1777, after the Battles of Trenton and Princeton," invokes a tone of mythic prophecy still common in military tributes today.

The Stocktons socialized with prominent families of the immediate area, such as the Burrs, whose son Aaron Burr, Jr., would become Vice President of the United States, and William Franklin, Royal Governor of New Jersey. During the British invasion of Manhattan on September 15, 1776, Major Aaron Burr, Jr. served as an aide to General Israel Putnam. By August 11, 1778, Burr rose to the rank of lieutenant colonel and become an aide to General Washington. In 1768 William Franklin appointed Richard Stockton to the Governor's Council and in 1774 named him to New Jersey's Provincial Supreme Court. A moderate, he would ultimately opt for separation and be selected as a delegate to the Continental Congress and signer of the Declaration of Independence.

The New Jersey legislators convened in Nassau Hall, at the College of New Jersey, in Princeton, on August 30, 1776 to select a chief executive. Two names came quickly to mind: Richard Stockton of Princeton and William Livingston of Elizabeth.

Stockton seemed an ideal choice. Scion of a notable
New Jersey family, he was a distinguished young
lawyer and was fervently liberal. The vote split
evenly on the first ballot, but later
in the day the legislators chose
Livingston as wartime governor. As
commander of the New Jersey
Militia, Brigadier General Livingston
was descended from a celebrated
New York family of Scottish
Dissenters. Indeed, almost half of
the signatories of the Declaration of
Independence were of Scottish

ancestry. Livingston would later become an itinerant
with a price on his head. "Not a pleasant thought,"
Jane commented. "How risky to be New Jersey's first
non-colonial governor," she said.

**Nassau Hall as it
appeared in 1874.**

As social leaders of Princeton, the Stocktons' home
was a center for activity for the College of New
Jersey, the name by which it was known for 150
years, (it later became Princeton University).
Chartered in 1746 by Presbyterian Jonathan
Dickinson, Pastor at Elizabeth, and Aaron Burr, Sr.,
Pastor at Newark and several other New Jersey
churches, it was the fourth oldest institution of
higher education in British North America and the
oldest in New Jersey. Of the first six College of New
Jersey graduates in 1748, five became Presbyterian
ministers. The sixth, Richard Stockton, became a
lawyer.

In 1762 Stockton headed a group of townspeople
who helped build the First Presbyterian Church (later
to become the Nassau Presbyterian Church) on land
owned by the college. When Sir William Howe's
forces under Major General Lord Charles Cornwallis
arrived in Princeton on December 7, 1776, soldiers
stripped the pews and galleries for firewood, which
they burned in the sanctuary.

After the Battle of Princeton on January 3, 1777,

Nassau Hall in Princeton was named after King William III, Prince of Orange-Nassau, depicted in this painting by Godfrey Kneller.

both the church and the nearby Nassau Hall, built in 1756, served as barracks and hospital at different times for both the Continental and British troops. Nassau Hall, the large stone building of Princeton's college, was named at the request of Royal Governor Jonathan Belcher in memory of King William III, Prince of Orange-Nassau. He was from Nassau, a former duchy in Western Germany, now a part of the state of Hesse. It was the setting during the Battle of Princeton for the last stand of some 200 British soldiers, who were garrisoned there until an artillery battery led by young Captain Alexander Hamilton dislodged them. A cannonball reputedly fired by Hamilton at Nassau Hall neatly decapitated the painting of King George II, convincing the Redcoats inside to surrender. (The portrait of George II was later replaced by *George Washington at the Battle of Princeton*, painted in 1784 by Charles Willson Peale).

Hamilton, an illegitimate child born on Nevis in the West Indies and orphaned as a boy, had made his way to New York as a teenager and studied law under Elias Boudinot at his office in Elizabeth. Short, handsome, witty, debonair, and fatally attracted to women, he had the self-possession of a military man. He later proved his mettle, assuming a distinguished place at the bar of the State of New York. Jane was impressed with Hamilton's adventurous spirit.

Earlier in 1776, the first Legislature of the State of New Jersey had convened in Nassau Hall. At about the same time Hamilton attained the rank of Lieutenant Colonel, and was appointed to Washington's staff. Later, our first President named him as Treasurer of the United States.

Having seen the Nassau Presbyterian Church close to Nassau Hall on the Princeton University campus, Jane wanted to learn more about the Presbyterians. I explained that they were largely of Scots-Irish ancestry, were united against Anglican Loyalists, and that they were in the forefront of the independence movement. Some of the Scots-Irish had emigrated from the northern part of Ireland in 1730. They had passed down stories to their children of atrocities inflicted in Ireland and Scotland by the government of King Charles I. By 1770, one-third of the churches in New Jersey were Presbyterian.

Elected to the Continental Congress in 1776, the Reverend John Witherspoon, along with Richard Stockton of the Princeton Presbyterian congregation, were signatories of the Declaration of Independence. Witherspoon served as President of the College of New Jersey and Pastor of the First Presbyterian Church for a quarter of a century.

Unquestionably the leading Presbyterian statesman in America during the eighteenth century, Witherspoon provided leadership to the movement for the organization of the national Presbyterian Church. But the greatest impact of his leadership of the patriot cause was vividly evidenced by the testimony of John Adams. While a visitor to Morven on August 24, 1774, he described Witherspoon as a "high a Son of Liberty as any man in America." (The Sons of Liberty was formed in response to the Stamp Act of 1765.) His strong advocacy of civil and religious liberty provided the intellectual foundation for his support of American independence. "Imagine being in Princeton with both Adams and Witherspoon together," Jane said.

John Adams could vividly recall the Monday of July 1, 1776. At the Pennsylvania State House, about four o'clock in the afternoon, while he was speaking, the hallway door flung open as three men entered, booted, spurred, with rain dripping from their coats. The radical members from Jersey had arrived and had come to vote for independence.

Speaking for New Jersey, Judge Richard Stockton asked to hear the affirmative argument once more before the vote should be taken in Committee of the

This painting, by Alonzo Chappel, shows Alexander Hamilton in the uniform of the New York Artillery. Legend has it that a cannon ball shot my Hamilton at the British in Nassau Hall "decapitated" a portrait of King George II.

Rev. John Witherspoon

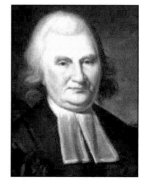

A moment of Patrick Henry's fiery rhetoric depicted by artist Peter F. Rothermel in an 1851 oil painting.

Whole. Rising to speak, John Adams patiently went through the argument again, while the opposition and two of their speechmakers made both vehement and abusive remarks.

President Witherspoon stepped boldly forward. His coat was soaked from the rain and his clergyman's bib lay wilted on his chest. He declared, "The distinguished gentleman from Massachusetts remarked as we came in that the colonies are ripe for independence. I would like to add that some colonies (presumably looking pointedly at Alsop of New York who had not yet decided for independence) are rotten for the want of it!"

This deliberate and agonizing debate preceding the decision of the thirteen colonies to declare their independence most likely typified the true feelings of the majority of the population, more than the polarizing rhetoric of John Witherspoon or Patrick Henry. In this case, it was as if all the passionate oratory of Virginia's Patrick Henry and all the overt rebellion of John Adams and the New Englanders had melded together in the persons of Stockton and Witherspoon. The ringing preamble of the Declaration of Independence, drafted by Thomas Jefferson, declared it "self-evident" that "all men are created equal," and were endowed with the "unalienable" rights of "life, liberty, and the pursuit of happiness." To this noble end, the Congressional delegates pledged their lives, their fortunes, and their sacred honor.

In early July of 1776, the war had certainly become a reality for the citizens of New Jersey. With the arrival of Admiral Lord Howe's fleet in New York Bay, the patriots only had access to New England by way of the Hudson River. As a precautionary measure, they constructed Forts Lee and Washington on opposite sides of the river, to guard it against British intrusions. Fort Lee was named for General Charles Lee, second in command to Washington, and

Fort Washington for the Commander-in-Chief himself. By this time, the king and his representatives felt that the time had come for Great Britain to put an end to the American insurgency. As October turned into November a crisis threatened, and New Jersey appeared doomed for an inevitable invasion. Jane was surprised to learn that the British army had actually invaded New Jersey.

The British and Hessian soldiers were well equipped and professionally trained. The inexperienced Americans were unable to hold or defend their forts. Built on Manhattan's highest point, 230 feet above the Hudson River, Fort Washington fell to British troops on November 16, 1776. Both Washington and Nathanael Greene deeply regretted their decision not to have abandoned it earlier. Their lack of foresight cost was 53 killed, 96 wounded, and 2818 soldiers taken prisoner. The British captured large quantities of ammunition, supplies and cannon, striking yet another blow to the American defense.

General Charles Lee, second in command of American troops after George Washington, and namesake of Fort Lee.

Just two days later, Washington evacuated his troops from Fort Lee, located about 300 feet above the Hudson River on the New Jersey side. The subsequent British invasion of New Jersey was inaugurated on November 20 under the command of Major General Lord Charles Cornwallis. In the predawn darkness, he maneuvered some 6,000 troops across the Hudson in whaleboats. Following a steep, little-used path that sloped up the rocky Palisades at about a 45-degree angle, the British scaled the cliffs of Closter's Landing in Bergen County, New Jersey. This daring attack was very much like the one Howe had led up the slopes of Quebec in the French and Indian War. In the speedy retreat that followed, General Nathanael Greene's garrison was forced to abandon Fort Lee and leave behind their badly needed tents, cannon and supplies.

General Nathanael Greene painted from life by Charles Willson Peale in 1783 .

Outflanked and out manned, General Greene promptly led his poorly clothed and ill-equipped Continental Army of 3,400 men west across the Hackensack River on November 21, crossing at historic New Bridge Landing by the Jan Zabriske House at River Edge. With the British in close pursuit, the army was once again forced to leave behind their much-needed supplies. Washington had hoped to make a stand at the landing, but the determination of the British did not permit him enough time. Escaping over the narrow bridge, the Americans made a hasty retreat. Washington rode at the rear of the column, a fact long remembered by James Monroe, a newly arrived eighteen-year-old lieutenant from Virginia. "So James Monroe, our fifth President, was a revolutionary, too; I never knew that," Jane said.

Washington was concerned about the health of his men and about rumors of a British invasion force landing at Perth Amboy. British General Sir Henry Clinton had in fact argued that he and his forces should land at Perth Amboy and thus outflank, destroy and cripple the rebels before the onset of snow.

Heading southeastward to Newark in a driving cold rainstorm, with the enemy in hot pursuit, the Americans arrived in that city on November 23, and remained there until the 28th. They continued their two-and-a-half week "Long Retreat" through Elizabeth, New Jersey's first English settlement, through Rahway and on to Woodbridge.

Continuing along what is now Route 514, (the King's Highway) they crossed the Raritan River at Piscataway's river port, called "Raritan Landing," at the Falls of the Raritan. They continued into New Brunswick on the morning of November 29, clattering across the 1772 wooden Landing Lane Bridge (New Jersey's first covered bridge, and one of the earliest in the nation). At the foot of Hamilton

Street townspeople grimly watched as flames partially engulfed that structure after Washington ordered it burned to help keep the British at bay.

Today one can read a site marker on Rutgers' Queen's College campus, near Kirkpatrick Chapel, which describes how Washington spent three days and two nights at Cochrane's Tavern in New Brunswick. The unheralded, nineteen-year-old Captain of New York Artillery, Alexander Hamilton, who had left King's College (now Columbia University) to serve the cause, now proved his mettle. His artillery company cannoned British and Hessian soldiers on the opposite side of the Raritan River who had appeared on the scene by late Sunday afternoon of December 1. Their cannonade fended off the approaching British army long enough for Washington to put together his New Brunswick strategy. "Three cheers for Hamilton," Jane exclaimed!

Washington sent troops ahead to scour the banks of the Delaware River for boats—especially the big Durham boats—from as far north as Coryell's Ferry (present day Lambertville) and as far south as Burlington. He ordered them to be transported to Trenton, twenty-six miles southeast of New Brunswick, for his strategic crossing of the Delaware. Washington directed that all other boats were to be removed to the west side, out of the reach of the enemy. As the British troops arrived in New Brunswick the next morning, they discovered that the Americans had already departed. Washington had marched his army of 3,400 bedraggled troops through the night, reaching Trenton by December 2. The exhausted army paused by the cold waters of the

A future U.S. President, James Monroe was an eighteen-year-old lieutenant from Virginia during the American's retreat across the Hackensack River.

The Battle of Trenton, depicted here by Hugh Charles McBarron, Jr. in 1975, was a dramatic turning point for the Americans.

Delaware and boated over to the Pennsylvania side. Washington was derisively labeled by his foes as a master of "defeat and retreat."

Thomas Paine, an immigrant corset-maker from England who had spent the summer of 1776 in Perth Amboy with General Mercer's Flying Camp, joined Washington's little army at Fort Lee and limped along on the journey across New Jersey, scribbling in his notebook at every stop. His words, written under extreme duress, became the series of pamphlets titled "The American Crisis." Their stirring paragraphs, icons of American prose, begin: "These are the times that try men's souls. The summer soldier and the sunshine patriot will, in this crisis, shrink from the service of their country; but he that stands by it now deserves the love and thanks of man and woman."

Paine's writing proved all too true. More than 1,000 New Jersey and Maryland troops, whose enlistment period had expired, declared they were going home. Nothing could induce them to stay, not even in this hour of danger. On the last day of November, when the enlistments expired, General Greene declared the Jerseymen acted "scurrily," ignoring the fact that New Englanders and Southerners had also left the army as their enlistments had expired. Jane found all this very distressing.

Now that Washington and the remnants of his Continental Army had crossed the Delaware River at Trenton into Pennsylvania, the British invasion was complete. This first crossing was as grim as the more famous one of Christmas, 1776, but at least the troops were not vulnerable to further chase. Every boat for miles around had been rowed to the west side of the river at Washington's direction.

"These are the times that try men's souls..." George Washington used Thomas Paine's words from *The American Crisis* to inspire his troops in the fraught hours before their pivotal Christmas crossing of the Delaware River.

With Washington and his troops on the western shore of the Delaware opposite Trenton, the state of New Jersey was now at the mercy of the British. Fearing the British would seize Philadelphia, the Continental Congress fled to Baltimore, remaining there until March, 1777. American troop morale was at a low point, and troop desertion became a major concern. "How difficult this must have been for Washington," Jane asserted.

"But on December 13, at Trenton, Sir William Howe made one of the fateful decisions of the war," I explained. Howe decided he and his army would retire to winter headquarters in Perth Amboy and New York, leaving only a token string of outposts in New Jersey.

By December 15, Howe had left Trenton and returned to Manhattan, settling comfortably in the elegant Beekman House. Safe in New York, he attended lavish parties, and, together with his mistress Elizabeth "Betsy" Loring, indulged in their penchant for gambling. Francis Hopkinson, one of New Jersey's five signers of the Declaration of Independence–and a musician and composer,

among his other talents–was hardly alone when he suggested in a popular ballad that General Howe's carrying on with his mistress had taken a toll on the British war effort. One verse in particular parodied Howe's soft lifestyle and his failure to pursue Washington aggressively:

> *"Sir William he, snug as a flea,*
> *Lay all this time a-snoring,*
> *Nor dreamed of harm as he lay warm*
> *In bed with Mrs. L____g"*

By December 19, the first of Tom Paine's "Crisis" essays was in circulation. Washington ordered it to be read to every regiment camped along the Delaware. Jane sensed how low Washington must have felt at this point of the war.

By December 20, Howe had Lord Cornwallis set up a string of seven garrisons–at Hackensack, New Brunswick, Kingston, Princeton, Trenton, Bordentown, and Burlington–to hold the central part of New Jersey for the winter. The main British army then moved back to the towns of New Brunswick and Perth Amboy.

By December 22, reports showed only 4,707 American soldiers fit for duty in the Pennsylvania encampment, a decline of more than 1,000 men in a period of two weeks. Washington glumly reported that many of his men were "entirely naked and most so thinly clad as to be unfit for service."

Returning to Morven on November 29, with the British pursuing the retreating Americans down the King's Highway in Princeton on December 3, the Stocktons reluctantly fled to Tory Monmouth County. Here in early December Richard Stockton was taken prisoner, handed over to the British in Perth Amboy and confined in the old Middlesex County Jail, on the corner of State and Market Streets.

On November 30, coincidental with Stockton's

arrest, Admiral Lord Richard Howe and General Sir William Howe, acting as peace negotiators as well as military commanders, issued a proclamation offering pardon to all who would submit to British rule and take an oath of allegiance to the king within sixty days. Thousands in New Jersey flocked to the British garrisons to declare their loyalty.

Richard Stockton was kept confined to Provost Prison in New York, and suffered brutal treatment in the poor conditions there. He was later released, with his health ruined, after accepting a pardon from British Commander General Sir William Howe. Stockton gave his "word of honour that he would not meddle in the least in American affairs during the war." Richard Stockton thus became the only Signer to recant his stance, marking, arguably, the lowest point of the American Revolution.

Morven

The Old Stockton Family

ust beyond the Battle of Princeton Monument in downtown Princeton, one of New Jersey's most celebrated historical communities, stands the imposing Stockton mansion, otherwise known as Morven. Recently restored, it was home to five generations of the Stockton Family, and it has been designated a National Historic Landmark by the National Park Service. It was the home of Richard Stockton, a signer of the Declaration of Independence. Its four large chimneys rise well above the roofline, framing the central portion and its two matching wings.

It was mid-afternoon in May when Jane and I arrived. A tangle of wisteria was still in bloom across the principal front entrance. The Executive Director, who greeted us at the door, had barely taken a breath when we announced that we had come to do a ghost investigation. "Ghosts, you say? I've nothing against ghosts, however, I've never seen one," was her comment. I replied, "I think a house with a ghost is much more valuable than a house without one! There's more to mystery than there is to fact."

Within the psychic community, it is well-known that buildings that have been recently renovated are ripe for haunting. The presence of ancient building materials could make such a structure a veritable magnet for ghosts, Jane explained. Researchers have investigated hundreds of reports of hauntings throughout the world, and if there is any pattern which can be determined, it is not geographic, socioeconomic or demographic–it is architectural. Morven has many tales to tell.

The tales of Morven are not only of its architectural splendor; they are of ghosts. So who are the ghosts of Morven? Jane Doherty, with her ability to communicate with the "other side" had come to uncover them. And uncover them she did!

The story of Morven comprises a chain of events extending over the better part of three centuries. Their characters include individuals who are largely forgotten (except in the record books of history), but who greatly influenced the destiny of New Jersey and the United States of America. While the mortals who dwelt here have long since departed, their spirit energy remains, still darkly overshadowing their posterity, as well as those who visit the venerable mansion.

As we entered the mansion, we could not help feeling a strange sensation of spirit energy around us. The people who visited the mansion and lived within its walls included many members of the influential class—founders and patriots, presidents and governors, clergymen, public officials and judges—the social, political, and educational elite of the day. All passed through the same principal entrance, which is almost the breadth of a church door, scraping their feet on the then-unworn threshold as they entered.

Here we learned of the vague and at times closely guarded stories of vaporous spirits who float through the hallowed halls, as well as other ghostly goings-on in this bustling, charming first White House of the United States. For it was here, in 1783, that Elias Boudinot, the President of the Continental Congress, lived when Princeton was the Capital of the United States. There was also another guest—the only visitor who is certain, at one time or another, to find his way into every human dwelling. When the patriarch of the Stockton family, Richard Stockton, the Signer, died in his room here, Death stepped across the threshold of the Morven mansion.

Richard Stockton's death was mystifying. Had he developed a cancer because of the hardships and brutal treatment he had received when imprisoned by the British in December of 1776, as was reported in

Designed by Frederick MacMonnies and Thomas Hastings and unveiled in 1922, the monument to the Battle of Princeton reads, "Here memory lingers to recall the guiding mind whose daring plan outflanked the foe and turned dismay to hope when Washington, with swift resolve, marched through the night to fight at dawn and venture all in one victorious battle for our freedom."

In addition to being
home to generations of
the Stockton family,
Morven served as home
to five of New Jersey's
governors between 1945
and 1982.

some nineteenth-century accounts? Or was it the emotional trauma he experienced when, to gain his freedom, he recanted his allegiance to the American cause, whose Declaration of Independence he had signed, leaving his reputation as a Revolutionary War leader in question?

With the British pursuing the retreating Americans down the King's Highway, the Stocktons fled Morven on November 29. Instead of following Washington's army to relative safety in Pennsylvania, they unaccountably sought refuge in Tory-controlled Monmouth County. Within two days, Richard Stockton was taken prisoner and handed over to the British in Perth Amboy. From there he was moved to the notorious Provost Jail in New York where the conditions for prisoners were very harsh.

In early January of 1777, Stockton obtained his freedom by accepting a pardon from British commander Sir William Howe. Having already resigned from the Continental Congress, he agreed to take no further part in the rebellion. This decision met with the disapproval of many supporters of liberty. In signing Howe's declaration, he gave his word of honor that he would not meddle in the least in American affairs during the war. Before the war had officially ended, Richard Stockton died in 1781, at the age of fifty-nine.

It was not our purpose to trace the subsequent generations of Stocktons who lived in the mansion. We were here to gather impressions of the spirits who continue to dwell here. In the dining room is a large, faded looking glass (mirror) fabled to contain within its depths all the shapes and emotions that had ever been reflected there, including Richard Stockton and his many descendants–some in the garb of babyhood, others in the full bloom of feminine beauty or manly prime, some saddened with the wrinkles of age. If only we could unlock the secret of that mirror, we could make it come alive with the departed Stocktons as they had shown themselves to the world. The mirror held the reflections of the family's past within its muted features–people enjoying happy times, perhaps carrying out some sinful deed, or enveloped in the crisis of life's bitterest sorrows.

Our tour began in the old west wing. Our guide throughout the investigation was a perfect skeptic, which made our visit all the more intriguing, for as we toured from room to room, Jane's impressions were corroborated by our guide's ample knowledge of the mansion's history.

In the eighteenth century, all food was cooked in a large kitchen-wing fireplace. Here in the west wing, Jane received the impression of the spirit of an African American woman busy preparing food and passing it on serving platters to a male butler. Oddly, the room is no longer recognizable as a kitchen. It has been greatly renovated, and is now the orientation room from which all house tours begin. Its walls contain portraits and exhibits that tell the story of the Stockton family.

Do the spirits of the kitchen servants still perform their duties in the kitchen at Morven?

Jane also received a very strong sensation of a woman named Sarah, who appeared nervous and worried. We were to later learn that the only Sarah who ever lived at Morven was Sarah Marks, who married John Potter Stockton (Commodore Robert Field Stockton's second son) on May 19, 1845. Most of what is known about the domestic affairs of the Morven family at this period comes from her diary. She was often depressed, and her diary hints at frequent quarrels with her husband.

Entering the dining room, we were impressed with its large and formal proportions. It is furnished with pieces from the Stockton family, as well as with china from the family of Richard Stockton's wife, Annis Boudinot. Unseen to our guide, Jane, in her mind's eye, saw the strong presence of a man, very anxious and very worried. He paced back and forth in front of the windows, sporadically looking out past the craggy limbs of the ancient trees that line the two main drives of the legendary mansion. Legend has it that his phantom silhouette, on occasion, appears to flash through the large wall mirror there.

John Potter Stockton was photographed sometime between 1860 and 1875 by either Mathew Brady or Levin Handy.

Jane also described troops moving on the highway in the distance, as the man deliberated about what he should do and how he should handle this upsetting and unexpected event. Could this presence be Richard Stockton making up his mind to flee to Monmouth County before the British arrived in Princeton in their pursuit of retreating American troops?

Jane then led the way into the grand entrance hall. Here she saw an elegant horse-drawn carriage pulling up the long horseshoe-shaped drive to the main entrance. A gentleman alighted, but it was only to offer his hand to a young girl. Her slender figure, not needing such assistance, lightly descended the carriage

steps, and made an airy little jump from the final one to the pavement below. She rewarded her cavalier with a smile, the cheery glow of which was seen reflected on his own face, as he re-entered the vehicle. The girl then turned towards Morven, giving a sharp rap on the door with the old iron knocker, and was welcomed inside by the lady of the house. A continual stream of guests kept arriving, all joining in the party. "They're going to have a ball," Jane said.

Perhaps the ghosts of these revelers still relive the fun of balls at Morven!

Moving into the morning room, Jane felt the presence of Annis Boudinot Stockton, now a widowed grandmother, seated in her favorite chair. She was being entertained by her grandchildren, all gathered around her playing games. Although she was a published poet, and correspondent of George Washington, she found that life had become more and more difficult. There was nothing bitter in Annis's poor old heart–she wished all persons well. But her own private wish was to be done with her life and laid in a quiet grave; things had never been the same since her Richard had died. Nevertheless, in the morning light, the grandchildren brought some of their cheery influence with them, smiling and laughing while in their playful antics.

During the happier times of her youth, Annis Boudinot Stockton was the lovely hostess of Morven, poet and correspondent of George Washington. A patriot in her own right, she was the only woman made an honorary member of the American Whig Society for her service during the Revolution. If her spirit really does still haunt her home, however, it may hint at a more melancholy old age.

Jane sensed that the children's smiles would first be a comfort to Annis, but then, inside her heart, would be a sob. It was as if she were saying to herself, "I can't continue to go through with it. I wish I were dead, and in the family tomb with all my forefathers! The world is too chill and hard, and I am too old, and too feeble, and too hopeless!" But the anxiety and misgivings that tormented her, whether asleep or in melancholy daydreams, seemed to vanish away as she heard the children laughing. Their energy would inspire her to get some breakfast and have perhaps have a second cup of tea.

Entering a room that was once the library, Jane felt the presence of an elderly gentleman of a remarkably dignified demeanor, passing slowly to the right of the mantelpiece. He stopped, having difficulty walking, as if he were tipsy. It was as if he was accustomed to a sad monotony in his life, isolated and withdrawn. Jane perceived him to be a person of influence and authority. In his youth, he had probably been handsome; at his present age, his remaining hair was too gray, his eyes too cold and his lips too closely compressed to bear any claim to good looks.

Our guide explained that the library was added to the mansion in the mid-nineteenth century, and had a secret staircase just to the right of the fireplace. Jane sensed this gentleman's presence ascending the secret stairs to avoid meeting with any intrusive guests. This same reclusive spirit has been suspected as the unseen entity that has emptied unfinished wine from glasses in the dark of the night before Morven became the official residence of five governors of New Jersey in the twentieth century.

Our tour would not be complete without a visit to the main staircase. Here Jane felt an icy chill around her legs when she stopped at the first landing. A spirit was definitely present. This landing also adjoins a shorter stair flight that leads to the east wing sitting room. "Someone is trying to get away; it's a woman."

Jane said. Former guests and staff members have reported chilling glimpses of her ghostly vision. Some have even felt a gentle pressure on the shoulder or the feeling that someone has just "walked" through them as they passed up this staircase.

In life, this woman would have descended this staircase to gain access to the garden by the door at its foot, Jane sensed. She would tend and trim the flowers for relaxation, and weed the occasional flowerbed. At other times, she would gather some roses and a few other flowers that possessed either scent or beauty, later arranging them in a lovely flower vase. But now, within a scant moment, Jane sensed this woman's need to get away from a man with whom she has just had a violent argument and who had been rough with her. Jane saw her fleeing down the staircase to escape his brutality.

Does Sarah Marks Stockton's desperate spirit still flee down these stairs at Morven?

Could this be Sarah Marks Stockton's ghost? Her spirit, it is said, still walks the grounds and gardens of old Morven. If you listen closely, the sounds of her sobs may be heard from time to time. A letter from Mrs. S.H. Cheston to Helen Hamilton Shields Stockton, dated July 9, 1899, confirms that during her visit to Morven she saw a ghost in the east wing sitting room adjoining the main staircase at the first landing where Jane experienced an icy chill.

It had been a very eventful visit, indeed! We graciously thanked our hostess, and continued our visit to Princeton with a stopover at the Princeton Battlefield State Park and the Thomas Clarke House. As we left Princeton that day, buried deep within my thoughts was the history of the life of Richard Stockton and his residence, Morven. As Jane described her impressions of his spirit that day, I had been visibly shaken and wished there was something that could be done to put his spirit to rest. Hoping to visit Morven again, I sadly was sure he would still be there as he has been since he died on February 28, 1781.

Triumph

The Triumph of Courage & Conviction in New Jersey

Chaos and fear gripped the populace of New Jersey during as the month of December 1776. The New Jersey Provincial Assembly dissolved, and marauding bands of Tories, British, and Hessians roamed and plundered the prosperous countryside between Trenton and Newark. Cunningly, and with little organization, Jersey men struck back with their own version of guerrilla warfare. Often burning Tory houses, they hung or shot citizens suspected of giving comfort to the other side. Striking under the cover of darkness, patriots made the royal forces uneasy, capturing those who tried to confiscate crops and animals while foraging for themselves through the Jersey hinterlands.

King George III gave little heed to the Declaration of Independence. Neither he nor his cabinet was inclined to take the warfare in the colonies too seriously. To him, it seemed incredible that a group of mere provincials could defy a powerful country like Great Britain successfully. He and his political peers had never served in America. (In fact, George III had never been a soldier, nor traveled to America, any more than he had set foot in Scotland or Ireland). Thus they had little comprehension of the difficulties of maintaining an army in hostile territory. Likewise, they had small respect for the military ability of the Americans. Their position simply was to compel the submission of the colonies by force of arms. Jane could sense how far removed King George III was from all that was transpiring in the American colonies.

Now sincerely intrigued by New Jersey's key role in the American Revolution, Jane asked me to tell her the story of Washington's famous crossing of the Delaware. Because this event happened in New Jersey, this was one story she vaguely remembered from her high school days.

After hundreds of Jersey men signed oaths of allegiance to King George III, Sir William Howe returned to New York's pleasures and Lord Cornwallis booked passage for England to reunite with his ailing wife, agreeing to return in the spring, "if there is another campaign which we doubt." Cornwallis was a true eighteenth century English aristocrat, born to wealth, position and influence. Tall and overweight, as was the fashion, he was devoted to his wife, whom he missed dreadfully.

Assuming the war to be waning, Charles Cornwallis, 1st Marquess Cornwallis, wanted to return to England and his ailing wife, whom he greatly missed.

With the British invasion of New Jersey complete, and the sad rabble of Washington's soldiers so unfit for service, how did the Commander-in-Chief of the Continental Army mount the courage and conviction to continue his campaign for independence? Safely across the Delaware and encamped in Pennsylvania by December 8, Washington needed to muster all the help he could get.

Two sources of relief soon presented themselves. The first was the arrival of Major General Charles Lee's men from Basking Ridge under the command of General John Sullivan, effectively doubling the size of Washington's army. On December 13, British dragoons had captured the forty-five-year-old Lee, the second ranking officer in the American Army, (who had failed to obey Washington's orders to retreat) as he enjoyed a late breakfast at the Widow White's Tavern in Basking Ridge. Taken prisoner by the most dreaded of British officers, Lieutenant Colonel Banestre Tarleton, the zealous cavalry commander, Lee was removed to New Brunswick and then to New York. There he was installed in a suite of rooms at City Hall, where fifty men constantly guarded him. His overseer, Lieutenant Colonel "Bloody Ban" Tarleton, as he was called, later boasted that he had slaughtered more men and raped more women than anyone in America.

Banastre Tarleton has been remembered for allegedly firing upon surrendering Continental Army troops at the Battle of Waxhaws, earning the nickname "Bloody Ban."

Major General Lee, Washington had confided to his

Johann Gottlieb Rall fought in the War of the Austrian Succession and participated in campaigns in Bavaria, on the Rhine, in the Netherlands, and Scotland. He fought in the Seven Years' War (French and Indian War) and was involved in many of its battles. From September 1771 until August 1772, he was in Russia, fighting for Catherine the Great under Count Orlov in the Fourth Russo-Turkish War.

brother, "is the first officer in military knowledge and experience we have in the whole army. He is zealously attached to the cause, honest and well-meaning but rather fickle and violent I fear in his temper." The Mohawk Indians had formed a similar impression twenty years earlier when Lee married a chief's daughter and fathered twins with her. Abrasive and hot-tempered, his Indian name was Ounewaterika, or "Boiling Water."

Washington's second source may have been information received from his faithful spy, John Honeyman, of Griggstown, a small village in Somerset County on the Millstone River. Records of spies were not carefully maintained, in order to protect their identities. However, a Honeyman family legend related at the Centennial of the Declaration of Independence in 1876 reported that Honeyman, posing as a British spy, informed Washington of the impending movement of the main British army back to New Brunswick and Perth Amboy by December 20. Honeyman also informed Washington that Colonel Johann Gottlieb Rall, commander of a band of Hessian mercenaries in Trenton, had failed to secure Trenton, as ordered by Cornwallis. "Spies! How intriguing," Jane commented.

Rall was a sturdy, able career soldier, and at age fifty-six, a senior army officer. His command at Trenton had been conferred in recognition of his valor in leading the Hessians at White Plains and Fort Washington. Trenton, only thirty miles north of Philadelphia, was the foremost British post held by Hessians. (Situated at the head of the navigable stretch of the Delaware River at the Falls of the Delaware, the first settlement was made about 1679; it was situated at the southern terminus of the most popular overland access route across New Jersey).

The legend is that Honeyman, returning across the Delaware River to Trenton, convinced Colonel Rall that the Continental Army was in a hopeless condition—hungry, cold, with no shoes and on the verge of mutiny. This was not far from the truth. Washington realized that quick action was needed. His men had enlisted for short terms, and many of them were due to leave for home at the end of 1776. In fact, on December 20, Washington hastily wrote to Congress that "Ten days more will put an end to the existence of our army."

The stage was set; Washington planned a Christmas night strike. He chose the presumed sanctity of Christmas as a cover to throw the Trenton Hessians off guard. His plan called for three divisions to cross the icy Delaware simultaneously—one at Trenton Ferry, another at Bristol, and the third at McConkey's Ferry House in Pennsylvania, eight miles north of Trenton. As snow and hail fell in the predawn darkness of December 26, only the third division, consisting of Washington and his units under Major General Nathanael Greene, Major General John Sullivan's Divisions and their Brigades, and Colonel Henry Knox's Regiment of Artillery, including eighteen field cannon and fifty horses or more, were successful. "Unknowingly," I commented, "Washington engaged the enemy with only a third of his forces." "Imagine how risky this mission was," Jane said.

A former bookshop owner, Henry Knox proved a masterful artillery commander. He would go on to serve as President Washington's Secretary of War.

A replica of Emanuel Gottlieb Leutze's famous painting *Washington Crossing the Delaware*, a 12-foot by 21-foot canvas painted in 1851 in Dusseldorf, Germany at the artist's studio near the Rhine River, is located in the New Jersey State Museum in Trenton. The work—an icon of our nation—may be the most recognized piece of historic American artwork. Leutze was a German who never saw the Delaware River or a Durham boat, as depicted in his painting. These big husky boats, built in northern Bucks County, Pennsylvania to haul pig iron, were used for generations of commerce on the river. They had a very shallow draft, and could float in about two and a half feet of water, even fully loaded. About eight feet wide,

they ranged up to sixty feet long. Poling, not rowing, propelled them forward.

Two Presidents-to-be crossed the river with Washington—James Madison and James Monroe. John Marshall, who would later become Chief Justice of the United States Supreme Court, as well as rivals Aaron Burr, Jr. and Alexander Hamilton, were also in the boats. A "storm of wind, hail, rain and snow" dangerously delayed the crossing, which finally landing at Johnson's Ferry in New Jersey. By 4 a.m., 2,400 Americans in two columns began their nine-mile march to Trenton.

Of the 30,000 or so German mercenaries that served in America for King George III, sixteen thousand were from Hesse-Cassel. (Present Hesse is a state in Germany just slightly larger than New Jersey). Hessian auxiliaries, fighting for the British, were placed in the forefront of every important battle in which they were engaged.

Beaten by their officers with the broadside of swords if they attempted to retreat, and made to do the menial tasks of their British overseers, their fate was a particularly cruel one. With no real interest in the outcome of the military struggle, and unfamiliar with the theory of "liberty" for which the Americans were fighting, it is no wonder that they often proved unfaithful, and deserted the army. At the war's end, some seven thousand Hessians remained in America.

On Christmas of 1776, the Hessians were stationed at the Trenton Barracks. Built in 1758 for British soldiers during the French and Indian War, it was to later function as a hospital for the Continental Army in 1777. These barracks were one of five built by the British in New Jersey, with the largest one being in the provincial capital of Perth Amboy. The Trenton Barracks is the only one still in existence today. "How fortunate we have this barracks to see," Jane said. I then explained that a replica center section of the barracks that once stood in New Brunswick is at the East Jersey Olde Towne village in Piscataway, just over the Raritan River from New Brunswick.

Leutze's painting of Washington's crossing of the Delaware may be the best known, but it certainly was not the only representation. Thomas Sully created this image in 1819 of Washington directing his troops.

Partially hidden by driving sleet, advance units of Washington's forces pushed past amazed Hessian pickets on the outskirts of town. By 8 a.m. on December 26 they had slammed into Trenton and routed some 1,400 dazed Hessians. In a mere forty-five minutes of fighting the Americans killed or wounded 106 men, and in less than two hours captured thirty officers, 918 prisoners, 1,000 muskets and rifles, six cannons, six wagons, and 40 horses. Another 500 soldiers managed to escape.

Colonel Rall was awakened to the sound of gunfire, and he fought bravely to rally his troops. During the fierce battle that ensued on the streets of Trenton, he fell, mortally wounded, approximately where the Trenton Battle Monument now stands. He was carried to his headquarters at the Stacy Potts House on King Street, where he died soon thereafter. Moved by this

Great Britain hired 30,067 German mercenaries to help fight in America. Out of these, 16,992 came from Hesse-Kassel, a principality of northern Hesse. This led to them being known collectively as "Hessians." These reenactors are dressed in the mitred helmets characteristic of the Hessians.

Gordon Bond

story, her eyelids drooped, and the ghost of a sob rose to the roof of her mouth as Jane felt the heaviness of the shocked dismay of Colonel Rall at having been caught so unexpectedly.

Washington would later write, "Finding from our disposition that they were surrounded and that they must inevitably be cut to pieces, they agreed to lay down their arms...Our loss is very trifling indeed, only two officers and one or two privates wounded." One of the officers wounded was Lieutenant James Monroe, later to become the fifth President of the United States.

The defeat of the Hessian force at the Battle of Trenton was a small but vital conquest, as the first notable triumph by the Continental Army and one of George Washington's most incredible military victories. It was reminiscent of the attacks at the Battle of Bunker Hill and at Dorchester Heights, the combination of which routed the British from Boston forever. When the news of Trenton reached Sir William Howe in New York, he was stunned. He responded immediately by canceling Cornwallis's trip home to England, and by ordering him and 8,000 of some of the finest troops to return at once to New Jersey to "bag the fox."

Cornwallis landed with his troops at Perth Amboy, and some 8,000 men quickly marched fifty miles west. By January 2, 1777, Cornwallis and his army were encamped at Princeton.

The victory at Trenton was also strategic, for it served to boost the morale of a dwindling and dispirited Continental Army and to galvanize the resolve of those Americans who still believed in

America's war for independence. Recognizing that Trenton could not be held against counterattack, Washington quickly returned along the same icy roads, and crossed the Delaware River at Johnson's Ferry into Pennsylvania. Jane was impressed with Washington's amazing courage.

A monument to General Hugh Mercer, who was killed at the Battle of Princeton, stands before the Thomas Clarke House at Princeton Battlefield State Park.

After the previous week's surrender by the Hessians, the British regrouped and retook Trenton, believing, with good reason, that they had lured Washington into a trap. But Washington escaped their ambush; if he had not, his army, and the cause that it stood for, might never have survived.

Washington did precisely what the British felt he could not do. On December 30, he started crossing the Delaware River again for the fourth time just south of Trenton, completing the crossing the next day. The river was so choked with ice that part of the crossing could be easily made on foot. He drew up his forces on a low ridge along the south side of the Assunpink Creek. "This part of the story I never knew," Jane said.

Before going to visit the Thomas Clarke House at Princeton Battlefield State Park, Jane then next asked me to recount the story of that victorious event. On January 2, 1777, Washington's army of citizen-soldiers, in a daring counterattack under heavy fire, engaged the British in the Second Battle of Trenton, also called the Battle of Assunpink Creek (having occurred at the wooden bridge over the Assunpink Creek that runs through Trenton at the foot of Queen Street near the Delaware River).

Cornwallis moved his main army of 7,000 men away from Princeton (leaving a force of 1,000 men as a rear guard) and reached Trenton, ten miles away, on January 2 in the early evening. Prudently, he decided

William T. Ranney created this painting in 1848, which depicts George Washington rallying his troops at Princeton.

to wait for morning to attack Washington. Washington's 5,000 to 6,000 troops were a mottled assortment of men, varying in experience and discipline; many were shivering and hungry, with their bloodied bare feet wrapped in rags. Under the cover of night, their spirits swelled with pride. They moved horses and cannon around the British forces at Trenton, following little-known back roads, to attack Cornwallis's rear guard at Princeton. The Americans left only a small group of 500 New Jersey Militia at Trenton to hold the British at bay. This group's function was to serve as a decoy, keeping the campfires going and making noises of entrenching troops to deceive the British.

Advance troops under Brigadier General Hugh Mercer reached Stony Brook (about two miles outside of Princeton) at sunrise, where they engaged the rear guard of Cornwallis's troops who were en route to Trenton. The nearby Stony Brook Friends Meetinghouse (built circa 1760, and still in use today), sheltered the wounded after the Battle of Princeton, and contains the unmarked graves of some of the soldiers killed in the battle as well as the unmarked grave of Richard Stockton, Signer of the Declaration of Independence.

General Mercer, the senior American officer, was bayoneted seven times and beaten in the head. His troops, bloodied and in mass confusion, were in the process of retreating when Washington arrived with his main army. He regrouped the bewildered men and repulsed the attack, defeating three British regiments. Thomas Jefferson considered George Washington the best horseman of his age; that was certainly proven true this day.

Among the fiercest battles of its magnitude during the American Revolutionary War, the field victory at Princeton concluded the military campaign known as the "Ten Crucial Days." The site of the Battle of Princeton, fought on January 3, 1777, is known as Princeton Battlefield State Park, and is in Princeton Township. It is situated on some eighty-five acres, preserving the fields of the Clarke farms, the battlefield itself, and the Thomas Clarke House (built circa 1772), where General Mercer clung to life for nine days before dying. It also contains the common grave of twenty-one British and sixteen American soldiers.

This sketch of Hugh Mercer was made by John Trumbull as a study for his painting, "The Death of General Mercer at the Battle of Princeton."

Mercer County was later named in honor of General Hugh Mercer. The historic Mercer Oak once stood on the battlefield, near where General Mercer was mortally wounded. It was adopted as the emblem for Princeton Township, Mercer County and the Green Acres Program. Unfortunately, the tree itself succumbed to a high wind storm in the year 2000.

Cornwallis reached Princeton at noon, but it was too late. The Continental Army had already disappeared. Princeton, like Trenton, proved to be another morale-building victory, and these three victories revitalized the cause for American independence. The mighty Royal Army had been outwitted, outgeneraled, and outfought. "This story makes me so proud to be an American," Jane said.

Leaving Princeton with his army, Washington headed north to Kingston, crossing the Millstone River in the process. Today's four-arch stone bridge over the Millstone River was built in 1793 as a replacement for the wooden one which Washington's men were forced to destroy as they eluded the enemy. It is the oldest four-arch stone bridge still standing in New Jersey. On its wall is a stone marker "Kingston//Bridge//45 M to Phil//50 M to NY// 1798". "What a treasure this New Jersey landmark is," Jane said.

Here Washington, together with Greene, Knox and

This four-arch stone bridge was built in 1793 to replace the wooden one burned by Washington's troops to prevent being followed by the enemy.

other commanders, held another council of war, while on horseback, making a decision to proceed to Millstone, Pluckemin, and Morristown. This was another complete surprise for the British, who surmised that the Americans would make a forced march of nineteen miles on to New Brunswick, where the British supplies and military war chest of 70,000 pounds sterling were stored. Henry Knox thought that 1,000 additional soldiers could have "struck one of the most brilliant strokes in all history" at New Brunswick. Washington later stated that he was convinced that a successful attack on New Brunswick, with its stores and pay-chest, could have ended the war.

Instead, leaving Kingston, Washington's army trudged north, crossing the Millstone River once again at Griggstown, and camping overnight in the fields at the village of Millstone. The river's Indian name was Mattawang, which meant "hard to travel." Originally it flowed in the opposite direction, but during the last Ice Age its normal course was reversed, emptying it into the Raritan River a short distance below Finderne.

Just south of the Millstone village is the Van Doren House, where Washington and his staff stayed overnight. Today, visitors can drive the scenic road that follows along the Millstone River and Delaware and Raritan Canal, as Jane and I did. The next day, the army proceeded north on present Route 533, crossing the Raritan River at the Van Veighten Bridge, and on to Pluckemin.

Imagine the triumph the soldiers must have been feeling on January 4 when they reached Pluckemin. Here Washington ordered an overnight stay, to give his exhausted soldiers some rest. The next day he withdrew his 5,000 troops and marched north to build their winter encampment at Morristown, in order to regroup and rest through the winter months of 1777.

At Pluckemin the troops encamped along Chamber's

Brook, south of town. General Washington and the notable people with him–Dr. Benjamin Rush (one of Washington's surgeons and a signer of the Declaration of Independence), Generals Henry Knox, Nathanael Greene, and John Sullivan–all stayed at the original Fenner House. It is said that Washington wrote his report to Congress of the Battles of Trenton and Princeton in the front parlor of the house.

Washington and his staff spent the night at the Van Doren house, which still stands south of Millstone village.

Cornwallis enhanced his growing reputation as a poor prophet by assuring his superiors that the American commander "cannot subsist long where he is." Adding further to the irony of the fate that awaited the British in America, I told Jane the following anecdote about the coronation of King George III.

In an age that had given England such rousing patriotic songs as "God Save the King" and "Rule Britannia," in a nation that adored the ultimate expression of ritual and gorgeous pageantry, the coronation was a scene that could hardly be improved upon. By 1761, the British Empire extended from Canada, the American colonies, and the Caribbean to the shores of India. London was the largest city in Europe, and widely considered the capital of the world.

As His Royal Majesty King George III was about to leave Westminster Abbey, a large jewel fell from his crown, an omen, which was remembered in later years, when Great Britain lost the American colonies. The jewel was immediately recovered, but the colonies were not!

Part Three

Geography, History & Culture

The View from Washington Rock

On Flag Day, June 14, Jane and I had agreed to drive to Washington Rock in the Township of Green Brook. We left South Plainfield early in the afternoon for the short drive. Having become aware that I might become more sensitive to the internal energy we all possess, I was eager to ask Jane some more questions during our drive, and share with her the drama of history as seen in the spring of 1777 from Washington Rock.

"Why are some people more aware of a sixth sense while others are not?" I asked Jane. "Actually" she explained, "psychic ability is naturally inherent within all of us. When we develop our psychic ability, we have a higher sense of perception and a greater understanding of life to make better decisions and create a more positive life. I truly believe in the power of the mind, especially the power of positive thought. Somehow we influence fate by our thoughts and actions and paint a portrait of who we are."

It is certainly true that negative thoughts can rule our lives as compulsively as an addiction. The feelings of power we get from holding a dismal and gloomy outlook deprive us of the positive and enjoyable parts of life. If one expects the worst, one will not be disappointed. It would be like taking the driving trip we are taking today and only looking for trash and garbage in the ditches, while ignoring the beauty beyond. Indeed, what we see may be very real in one sense, but it is a very limited piece of the picture, I thought.

Jane then explained that our past choices bring about our present circumstances. Decisions about our current situations actually determine our future. "If you have a pessimistic attitude, you could falsely accept most bad circumstances in your life as unchangeable fate. Without hope and a more optimistic attitude, you risk attracting more negative circumstances, which you must act upon, thus creating a cycle of despair. Circumstances in life that seem negative can have a different meaning when you look back at the experience. After a lapse in time, a serious problem can be seen as a blessing in disguise," she said.

Diligently, with the patience of the schoolteacher she used to be, Jane explained that in Greek the word "psychic" is derived from the word "psyche". Psyche actually means soul or spirit. "Psychic experience teaches you there is more to life than just the physical world. Developing psychic ability is an awakening process," she said.

Jane then told me that she really had not planned on becoming a psychic. Driven by her desire to understand the psychic information she was receiving through images, symbols, thoughts and feelings, she sought the expertise of psychics. "Everyone's purpose in life is to discover their own unique self and personal path in life. Through self-awareness, psychic guidance, inner knowledge and observation you can achieve your purpose, or if you will, your destiny," she said. "Studying the paranormal taught me we are so much more than physical bodies. We have a unique spiritual self, which is part of a much greater plan. And we have an obligation to discover this uniqueness and develop our soul's full capacity to love, so our piece of the plan can fit into the bigger puzzle," Jane explained.

"What if more people embraced a belief system that accepted paranormal experiences and psychic ability as a normal part of human experience? Could adding these beliefs inspire greater inner peace in a person's life? Or could recognizing guidance in everyday life help others feel a closer connection to God? The answers to those questions had to be yes, because those benefits had already manifested for me. Nothing in life can be achieved without belief, trust and

confidence, including your own connection to the other side," Jane continued.

Certainly George Washington, I thought, must have been a positive person. While in New Jersey, he made many momentous decisions, and was perceptive and understanding both of people and circumstances. With limited resources and few troops, he took on the world's most powerful army while enduring many grim and anxious moments with amazing courage and purpose.

Within a short time, we had reached our destination. Jane marveled at the view from Washington Rock. Situated on the First Mountain of the Watchungs, these "Blue Hills" were called by the Indians "Wach unks," meaning "High Hills." I could not resist explaining that the basalt rock on which we were standing was part of a continuous lava flow extending from the Bay of Fundy in Nova Scotia to Northern Florida.

During the Jurassic Period, New Jersey lay near the center of the supercontinent of Pangaea, which encompassed all of North and South America, Europe, Africa, Australia, Antarctica, and India. As Pangaea began to split apart, massive flows of lava occurred, which resulted in formations of basalt, a type of

The lava flows that created the Atlas Mountains of northern Morocco appear to be the same as those that created the Watchung Hills some 400 million years ago, when the regions were joined. This photograph shows Jbel Toubkal in Toubkal National Park.

solidified lava. Dating and chemical analyses of volcanic eruptions of lava flows in Morocco's Atlas Mountains have shown a striking match between the timetable of eruptions there and those of North America, as the continents split apart 360 to 400 million years ago. "You can never completely predict what may lie beneath your feet," I said. "This could very well be African rock!"

Jane was quick to add that our entire species is a very recent passenger on this spaceship Earth, at least when compared to the volcanic eruptions that formed these rocks beneath us. We have had a busy time of it, for the few thousand years that there have been enough of us in residence to make a difference. Measured in geologic time, we have barely entered the history books of the planet, particularly if our time on Earth is gauged by its estimated age of 4.5 billion years.

On that warm June 14 afternoon, with barely a cloud in the sky, and the sun streaming down on us, it seemed that we could see forever across the clear horizon. In the distance was New York City, Staten Island, Raritan Bay, and Sandy Hook. Gazing out across our 30-mile panoramic view, we could see the long ridge of the Atlantic Highlands in Monmouth County (its hills mark the highest elevations on the Atlantic coast between Maine and Florida) separating New Jersey's inner and outer coastal plains.

Before us we could see the great expanse of New Jersey's Piedmont Plateau, especially Sand Hill in South Brunswick and Poplar Hill at the heights of Edison, two of Middlesex County's highest elevations. Moreover, there was Perth Amboy, the Colonial Capital, and New Brunswick, the British field headquarters, both strongholds of the British troops in New Jersey in 1777.

The British, from their position at Brooklyn Heights in 1777, could take in a vast panorama to their west, including all of New York City, the harbor, the rivers, the long low hills, and the Watchung range of New Jersey, where we were now standing. It was one of the grandest prospects to be seen on the entire Atlantic seaboard.

Taking in this marvelous view, I explained that the first European settlers of these Jersey Midlands were the inheritors of a struggling merchant tradition. This had been set in motion as early as 1498 when John Cabot had sighted the Jersey coast for his King, Henry VII of England. The Florentine, Giovanni da Verrazano, who dropped anchor off Sandy Hook in his ship the *La Dauphine* in the spring of 1524, followed Cabot. Verrazano explored the Raritan and Hudson Rivers for Francis I, the King of France. In 1525, Esteban Gomez also explored this coast for the King of Spain, further confirming that this continent was part of a New World, and not Asia.

Giovanni da Verrazano arrived at Sandy Hook in 1524 while exploring the Raritan and Hudson Rivers.

As early as 1542, French fur traders were exploring the Hudson all the way up to what would later become Albany. Here they established a trading post, thus alerting both the Dutch and the English to the profitability of the French fur trade. There can be little doubt that the natives of New Jersey (called "Indians" by these early explorers who thought they were off the coast of India), had seen the ships of Cabot, Verrazano, Gomez, and the French fur traders, but it is Henry Hudson's first landing on September 4, 1609, at Sandy Hook, New Jersey, of which we have a record.

In 1909, on the 300th anniversary of Henry Hudson's discovery of the river which bears his name today, the Dutch sent the U.S. this replica of the ship *Half Moon.*

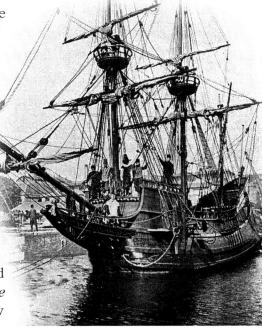

Henry Hudson was engaged to sail the eighty-ton *Halve Maen (Half Moon)* westward by

Hudson's voyage was paid for by the Dutch merchants of the powerful Dutch East India Company. Shown in this illustration are their Amsterdam shipyards. The *Vereenigde Oost-Indische Compagnie* held a twenty-one-year monopoly of colonization for the purpose of trade in Asia before going bankrupt in 1798.
Amsterdam Municipal Department for the Preservation and Restoration of Historic Buildings and Sites (bMA)

the great merchants of Amsterdam, who had already established highly profitable business relations in the Far East under the auspices of the Dutch East India Company. He was searching for a westward passage through North America, via either the Delaware or Hudson Rivers, to Cathay (China). His trip helped instigate the Dutch presence in New Jersey and New York, as the Dutch West India Company had rights to develop and administer the new territory known as Nieuw-Nederland. It was not until the early nineteenth century that the Northwest Passage quest was finally laid to rest.

The legacy of the Lenni Lenape "Indians" in the Raritan and Millstone River Valleys endures today. Place names such as Raritan, Assunpink, Watchung, Amboy, Metuchen and Mattchaponix are all derived from their language. The name Lenape has various meanings: "a male of our kind;" "our men;" "men of the same nation;" or "common;" "ordinary;" or "real" people. It does not mean "original people" in the sense that most writers have defined it. Jane was fascinated with all this background information and eager to learn more.

The great Raritan River and its tributaries, named after the Raritans, a tribe of the Lenni Lenape, lay spread out before us. First explored by Europeans in the 1500s, it is the largest river system in New Jersey, with headwaters in Budd Lake, at an elevation of 940 feet. It flows some eighty-five miles through the Highlands, Piedmont and Coastal Plain Provinces of north-central New Jersey, until it empties into Raritan Bay at South Amboy.

Over one thousand square miles of fertile valleys are drained by the Raritan River. The name Raritan comes from the Algonquian word *Laletan*, meaning "forked river." The South Branch is joined by the North Branch at a place known to the Indians as *Tucca-Ramma-Hacking* or "the meeting place of the waters."

Washington Rock, with its spectacular and distinctive topography and strategic location, made a valuable lookout point for General Washington during the First Middlebrook Encampment in June 1777 and the Battle of the Short Hills. It was pivotal to winning the events of the Second Middlebrook Encampment (1778-79), and indeed, some would argue, to winning the war itself.

Jane admitted that she was only vaguely aware of New Jersey's role in the American Revolution and wanted to discover more. I then explained that New Jersey was strategically located between the Continental Congress in Philadelphia and British-occupied New York, with the Delaware River in the west and access to New England by way of the Hudson River in the northeast. "So New Jersey was the major crossroads for

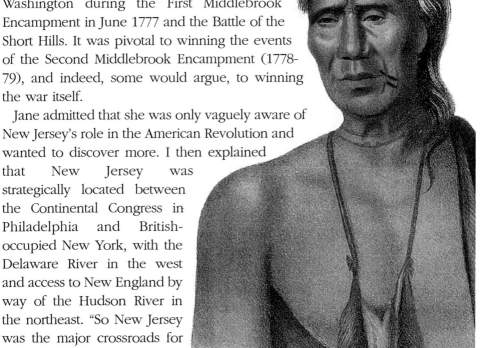

The Native Americans who inhabited New Jersey were members of the Lenni Lenape tribe. Below is a 1737 portrait by an unknown artist of Lapowinsa, Chief of the Lenape.

Infantry of the Continental Army.

the American Revolution for most of the eight years of the war," Jane said. Peninsula-like, New Jersey is surrounded by water; of its 480 miles of border, only 48 are land miles, I added.

Because New Jersey's Legislature was split in the seventeenth and eighteenth centuries between the Provincial Capitals of East and West Jersey–Perth Amboy and Burlington–good roads were required to serve the New York-Philadelphia route. The trip by stagecoach between these two cities took a little under three days, depending on the weather. But the mail coach, justly called the "Flying Machine," covered the same distance in only two days. For many years the only post offices in New Jersey were located in Perth Amboy and Burlington.

Journeying up and down the rivers and roads of New Jersey, troops enjoyed a greater degree of inter-colonial travel than in any other part of America. Several roads followed the Native American trails between the Raritan and Delaware Rivers. "And we're still a crossroads state!" Jane declared.

By 1750, New Jersey was well known for its produce, which was shipped to and through the port cities of New York and Philadelphia. It was already being called "The Garden" of the colonies. However, the corridor between these two cities, lying on the fertile Piedmont Plateau and Inner Coastal Plain, was not just suitable for farming. It was also the territory traversed by the British and Americans during one third of the Revolutionary War. Here they foraged from the local farmers for both themselves and their animals. Hay, oats, Indian corn, cattle, horses, and many other items of value disappeared in the twinkling of an eye whenever raiders appeared.

Families were abused, stripped of their beds and other furniture, and even of their wearing apparel. Wives and daughters were ravished, and rare was the slave who was not seized. The most battered of the thirteen colonies, the "Garden" colony would see the most raids and counter raids. Loyalists would invade patriot farms, and patriots in turn would seek revenge against neighbors who supported the king.

New Jersey, although it accounts for only 0.2 percent of the nation's territory, has a Revolutionary War heritage unequaled by any other state. It was home to a series of events between 1775 and 1783 that were crucial to the struggle for independence. An impressive array of historic houses, battlefields, landmarks, and monuments associated with the war are located throughout the state.

There were several major battles fought between the American and British armies in New Jersey, as well as many smaller engagements between units of the British army, partisan militias and individuals–more than in any other colony. Major policy decisions were made at the various encampments and headquarters located here, and the war itself produced more impact on its civilian population than in any other state.

As an important theatre of military operations, George Washington and the Continental Army spent more time here by far (almost half of the Revolutionary War), than in any of the other thirteen colonies. The daily hardships of the colony's soldiers and populace were the events that shaped a nation. New Jersey was indeed the "Cockpit of the American Revolution." "This makes me so proud to be from New Jersey," Jane said. "But there's much more to tell," I added.

Washington's success at Trenton and Princeton did much to enliven the spirits of the New Jersey Militia. By January 5, 1777, under General William Maxwell, they were able to drive the British down the Short

Paul Revere (above in John Singleton Copley's 1768 painting) is most remembered thanks to Henry Wadsworth Longfellow's 1861 poem, "Paul Revere's Ride." William Dawes (below) also rode, however, starting a cascade of spreading alarms.

Hills, through Springfield, Elizabeth and Rahway, and back to Perth Amboy. On February 1, General Maxwell's militia engaged foraging Royal Forces high on King Georges Post Road, near Fords, in the Battle of Spunk Hill. On February 23, fifteen hundred British soldiers marched out of Perth Amboy, and proceeded through Woodbridge to Rahway, only to be driven back again by Maxwell's forces.

On March 8, two thousand Redcoats left Perth Amboy to attack the rebels in their Rahway camps, only to find that they had walked into "a nest of American hornets" at an engagement in Woodbridge at Strawberry Hill. A final British surprise assault occurred on March 16 at Rahway, where several rebel soldiers were killed, and fifteen taken prison.

News of the first blows of the Revolution, struck at the Battles of Lexington and Concord on April 19, 1775, was spread by Paul Revere and other Massachusetts messengers, who had warned that the "Redcoats" were coming. The anniversary of these battles is still observed as a legal holiday–Patriots' Day– in Massachusetts and Maine (once part of the colony of Massachusetts).

Not until April 24, 1775 did a breathless post rider bring the astounding news to New Brunswick that British forces and the Minutemen of Massachusetts had clashed at Lexington five days earlier. When this news reached Woodbridge, Dr. Moses Bloomfield, a patriot leader, declared the inhabitants of his hometown were "determined to stand or fall with the liberties of America."

Unlike the Battles of Lexington and Concord, the army of Lord Cornwallis departed New Brunswick with much secrecy on the evening of April 12, 1777, avoiding the main roads to prevent the Americans from getting advance warning from spies. The next day his force, consisting of 4,000 British and Hessian

troops, made a surprise attack on the rebellious army of the colonies (500 to 600 strong) who were encamped at Bound Brook (originally called Boundary Brook).

The most dramatic and intense fighting came from two columns of British and Hessian troops. They crossed the Van Veighten Bridge and the stone-arched Queens Bridge, and routed the vastly outnumbered Americans from their redoubt–an earthen fort–constructed in the center of Bound Brook. General Sir William Howe reported to the British government that 30 rebels were killed, and 80 to 90 taken prisoner, including some officers. Three Jägers (Hessians) and four British infantry soldiers were wounded during the assault.

The attacks were swift and surprising, waking rebel General Benjamin Lincoln from his bed in the main house of the Philip Van Horne Plantation, and sending him fleeing through the countryside in his bedclothes. With American defenders fleeing into the hills, village residents (about thirty-five families) and farm dwellers

While the times and the neighborhood have certainly changed, General Lincoln is still roused from bed by a surprise attack each year during the annual Battle of Bound Brook reenactment events.
Gordon Bond

were at the mercy of the victorious British and Hessian troops, who ransacked the town and farmhouses before they marched back to New Brunswick.

With the news of the defeat at the Battle of Bound Brook clearly in mind, General George Washington left his winter headquarters at Jacob Arnold's Tavern on the public square in Morristown. On May 28, 1777, his troops mustered at their encampment at Morristown, and were quickly deployed along the east and west branches of Middle Brook and the south side of the First Watchung Ridge overlooking Bound Brook.

On June 1, 1777, General Washington wrote to Major General John Sullivan: "The people in this part of the state [Central Jersey] have acted with great spirit since our army has drawn into closer compass." The militia that General Maxwell had found so hard to organize was now becoming a large and effective force.

Spies had informed Washington that General Howe intended to capture the American capital at Philadelphia, in an effort to cut off and isolate the Southern colonies. From Washington Rock, Washington could see the movements of the British army as they deployed some 4,000 troops from occupied New Brunswick and another 13,000 from Perth Amboy. There they had filled all the houses of the city and made a barracks out of St. Peter's Church in Perth Amboy.

The once prosperous and beautiful port city of Perth Amboy, in 1777, had rapidly become an armed camp, as the genteel residences of the Proprietors, Perth Amboy's landed gentry, became overcrowded with soldiers. The quartering of troops in private homes was a source of friction and resentment in the colonies. Martial law deprived residents of their basic civil rights under the English Constitution by shutting down the courts and legislature. It also forced them to feed arrogant occupying soldiers and their dependents.

By June 13, 1777, General Howe had made a massive show of force, hoping to catch the Americans off guard and draw them out of the mountains into open battle on the flat land. But the night raids of the American soldiers and guerrillas, combined with roadside killings across the Somerset and Middlesex County plains, produced terror in the British, thus hindering their plan to capture the city of Philadelphia by land.

The Drake House stands in its original location in Plainfield.

Headquartered at the Drake House (built in 1746 in Plainfield), home of patriot Deacon Nathaniel Drake, Washington and his militia fought the Battle of the Short Hills over the entire Plainfield area–from Metuchen and North Edison to Scotch Plains and the Ash Swamp–between June 25-27, 1777.

The successful waiting-game strategy utilized by Washington and the Continental Army, combined with the threat of continued sniper warfare, goaded the British into full retreat. Howe took the Amwell Road (based on an old Lenni Lenape Indian Trail) from Somerset Courthouse (now Millstone) through New Brunswick to Perth Amboy on June 28, looting and burning houses along the way in New Brunswick, Perth Amboy and Piscataway.

Returning British forces also vandalized buildings in Woodbridge, where James Parker had established New Jersey's first permanent print shop. Though Parker had died in 1770, his son, Samuel Franklin Parker, served with General Nathaniel Heard and was likely present at the arrest of the last Royal Governor, William Franklin, at Perth Amboy. The younger Parker's home was burned to the ground–how the world had changed since the days when the fathers of Parker and Franklin had been friends! "How devastating for the people of that day; I feel their loss," Jane said.

By June 30, the Crown forces had removed themselves completely from Jersey soil, establishing camp in Staten Island. In New Jersey, moods grew brighter, tongues looser, and Tory sympathizers were

harder to find. Howe loaded his army on transports in hopes of gaining a hold on Philadelphia. Delayed by poor winds and stormy weather, Howe's armada of 267 ships, carrying 15,000 men, was forced to spend more than a month at sea before sailing up the Chesapeake. After landing at the head of the Elk River on August 25, they disembarked and headed on foot towards Philadelphia.

On June 14, 1777, the Continental Congress adopted our national colors. As Washington's army encamped at Middlebrook from May 28 to July 2, 1777, there was, tradition says, sufficient time for an official flag to have been brought there from Philadelphia. This encampment thus provided the first occasion to fly the Stars and Stripes, said to have been created by Betsy Ross. Today you can visit Washington's First Middlebrook Encampment site on Middlebrook Road in Bound Brook and see the thirteen Stars and Stripes flying there still.

"I've lived beneath Washington Rock in South Plainfield most of my life, and I never knew how important the spring of 1777 in New Jersey was to the cause of American Independence," Jane said. "No more. I envision that Washington's Revolutionary War visits to the lower valley of the Raritan River are about to receive new and important attention. The lower Raritan is on its way to becoming "Washington's Valley!" My heart pounded as Jane spoke. "Could this really be true?" I wondered.

Looking back for one last glance at the battlefield landscape we had just viewed, we reflected on those moments of painful confrontation and the overwhelming anxiety experienced during what had happened here. Then Jane, catching the scent of adrenalin in the air, and with a twinkle in her eye said, "Where are we off to next!" It was time to move on.

Adopted by the Continental Congress on June 14, 1777, the "Stars and Stripes" first flew over Washington's troops at the Middlebrook Encampment.

Old Stone Cottage

The Cutter Farm, Fords, New Jersey

*I*n 1655, Governor Petrus Stuyvesant made all of future New Jersey part of his colonial province of *Nieuw Nederland*. Roughly paralleling one of several major Lenni Lenape Indian Trails, the Dutch then laid out what is today Route 514, the first road built in New Jersey. A 1639 map, probably drawn by *Nieuw Netherland's* first surveyor-general, Andries Hudde, "The Manatus Map," clearly shows all of Middlesex County's present-day Perth Amboy, Fords and Woodbridge proper, opposite *Staten Eylant* (Island).

The Dutch people who settled *Nieuw Nederland* emigrated from a country where political and religious freedom was highly prized, popular education was nearly universal, and regard for law and order was held in high esteem. Early in the seventeenth century, the Dutch Republic had become a sanctuary for persecuted Protestants from other countries, most notably the English Pilgrims who sailed to Massachusetts aboard the *Mayflower* in 1620. On Monday morning, September 8, 1664, Petrus Stuyvesant, the sixth and last Director, surrendered the city of Nieuw Amsterdam to the English, officially ending almost fifty years of Dutch dominion in North America. New Jersey's official founding date was recorded when it was invaded, not when it was actually founded. Jane was fascinated to learn this.

Nevertheless, this capitulation did not mark the end of Dutch cultural influence, for the descendants of the original settlers lived much as they had before and, at least among themselves, continued to speak the Dutch language well into the nineteenth century. As late as 1866, Anne Rolff, wife of John Rutger Planten, Consul-General from the Netherlands to the Port of New York, wrote "The Dutch language has been handed down from parents to children

Petrus Stuyvesant, the peg-legged, anti-Semetic, last Dutch Director-General of the colony of New Netherland, is remembered for greatly expanding what would become New York City.

and sometimes as far as the fifth generation. I have personally observed this very often in New Jersey where my brother was settled."

Many of the descendants of New Netherlanders still reside in the Jersey Midlands. Among the more prominent Dutch families from the 17th century who still live in Middlesex County can be found these surnames (the parentheses indicates the Anglicization of the Dutch Name): Bayard, Bennett, Blaugutt (Bloodgood), Bergen, Bogardus (Bogart), Cortelyou, Dankers (Danker), Hardenburgh (Harden), Hewlett, Hulsart, Hulse, Jansen, Jonas, Koster, Lott, Low, Mandeville, Polhamus, de Potter (Potter), Provoost, Remsen, Roosevelt, Rutgers, Ryder, Schenk, Schuyler, Snediker, Staats, Strycker, Suydam, Tappan, Ten Broeck, Ten Eyck, Ter Heart (De Hart), Terhune, Vanderbilt, Vanderburgh, Van Cowenhoven (Conover), Van Dyke, Vander Heydens (Heyden), Vander Hoes (Hoes), Van Lieu, Van Syckel, Vanderveer, Van Voorhees, Van Winkle (Winkle), Vroom and Wyckoff. "And yet we never think of Middlesex County as being Dutch country, but it is!" Jane remarked.

After the English took control of the Dutch territories in 1664, Puritan settlers from Newbury, Massachusetts, would eventually settle the Fords section of Woodbridge Township on land just north of the Raritan River. The earliest name given to Fords (some time before 1669) was "Sling Tail" (perhaps from a brook by that name). The Inn of Samuel Ford (a Scottish name originally spelled Foard), for whom Ford's Corner and later Fords was named, stood on the corner of present day King Georges Post Road and Ford Avenue. The earliest inhabitants of Fords were farmers, who quietly tended their fields and herds. This agrarian society persisted well into the twentieth century, with Fords only becoming a suburban community after World War II. "How this area has completely changed," Jane said.

Under English rule, the original Indian path and former Old Dutch Road (present day Route 514 or

The walls of this decorative fish pond on the Old Stone Cottage property are formed by the foundations of an 18th century cow barn.

Main Street, Fords) became the King's Highway, the major road between New York and Philadelphia. Continuing west from Woodbridge Proper, Upper Main Street (Route 514) crosses both the New Jersey Turnpike and the Garden State Parkway, forming the crossroads of New Jersey's oldest road with its two most important arteries. With views of the "Blue Hills" of the Watchung Mountains to the north, it continues into the heights of Fords (among the three highest elevations in Middlesex County). Situated on the Wisconsin Terminal Moraine of the last great Ice Age, it passes by the one-time farm of the Cutter family, which used to encompass several hundred acres.

William Cutter, a nineteenth century Woodbridge farmer and clay merchant, was the proprietor of the Cutter Farm. He was descended from Richard Cutter of Massachusetts, who settled in Woodbridge in 1706, and who made his home near "Strawberry Hill." For most of the eighteenth and nineteenth centuries, the Cutter

Legend has it that Washington's troops satisfied their thirst with water from this stone well on the Cutter Farm.

family maintained their Fords farm.

The main house and barns at Cutter Farm all faced south in order to avoid harsh weather, as was the custom of the early Dutch and English builders in this area. The undeveloped land surrounding the few remaining acres of this estate residence is the largest extant farm property remaining in the township.

Throughout the Revolutionary War, local farmers lost horses, cattle and supplies of all kinds to the British. This would often occur on a daily or nightly basis, as farm after farm was looted of needed meat, milk and produce. These spoils were subsequently smuggled to Staten Island, New Brunswick or Perth Amboy.

At Cutter Farm, Olde Stone Cottage, built on the foundations of a circa 1690 stone barn, is indicative of the Pennsylvania-type barn in the New Jersey Piedmont. Originally, it was a two-floor banked structure built into a land bank (formed by the Wisconsin Ice Advance), allowing wagon access to both levels, a setup which is commonly called a "high-drive" in New England. Animals were kept on the first level, and the second level was used as storage space.

Barns were vitally important to New Jersey settlers from the time the Dutch first began arriving in the area. The foundations of at least two other barns are known to have existed at this site, in addition to the main dwelling of the same period. In the early morning hours of November 29, 1776, during Washington's "Long Retreat" across New Jersey, local legend has it that his thirsty troops drew water from the farm's deep fieldstone well, which still exists today. The fieldstone remains of a cow barn on the property have been converted into a charming fishpond and outdoor patio sitting area. These structures are the oldest existing examples in the greater Fords area.

A Native American encampment is also believed to have existed in the area. The psychic energy of a smoke-covered Indian mother on her knees holding the still body of her charred baby has been seen on several occasions. Indian arrowheads have also been found at various places on the property.

The second story of Olde Stone Cottage was converted into a servant quarters in Victorian times, and when the farm became a gentleman's country estate in the 1920s, the barn's first floor was adapted as a guest cottage. The last of the farm's land parcels was sold off in the mid-twentieth century and a major addition was completed on the cottage in 1960.

It was a recent mid-summer's evening, and Jane Doherty, who has been the focal point of hundreds, if not thousands, of séances, readings and ghost investigations over the past two decades, had come to Olde Stone Cottage to conduct a séance. As Jane entered the haunted entrance hall, she noticed a reflection in the oval brass-framed mirror of American Civil War vintage that hangs above a sixteenth century Spanish wall chair. I explained that a tall thin man in a long black waistcoat and a stovepipe hat (similar to the one that Abraham Lincoln wore) appears regularly, descending the main staircase into this hall. Jane sensed that his spirit energy was definitely present here, but could not determine who he was. "He has been sighted by many people," I explained.

"Spirits can attach themselves to objects," Jane uttered as she entered the large and imposing living room that overlooks the expansive rolling lawns and gardens. There were many antique objects to be seen and admired in this room: an early New England tavern table holds a Victorian oil lamp of American satin glass, eighteenth century brass candlesticks from Rhode Island, and old family Bibles of the Peck Family; Staffordshire statues on the mantelpiece help flank an 1869 Connecticut mantel clock; a Chippendale rosewood tea table holds a rare scrimshaw whale's tooth depicting James Lawrence, the American naval officer from Burlington, New Jersey, who, during the War of 1812, was in command of the frigate *Chesapeake*. (His famous cry "Don't give up the ship"

Séances date back to at least as early as 1760 in England when George, First Baron Lyttelton, published "Dialogues of the Dead." Spiritualism became popular in the U.S. during the Civil War as families longed for contact with sons, husbands and fathers who had been killed. A grieving Mary Todd Lincoln held séances at the White House after the death of her son. The slaughter of the First World War generated more interest, even attracting Sherlock Holmes creator Sir Arthur Conan Doyle. This photo dates from the 1920s.

was shouted as the British overwhelmed his ship). Several large oil paintings beautifully reflect the blues and mauve period colors of the room, including one of Perth Amboy's Parker Castle. Finally, several family portraits add life to the beauty of the room.

A dozen or so souls had gathered here, eager to experience psychic phenomena. The séance lasted about three hours, as one by one deceased friends and relatives "came through." Jane was able to call each spirit by name and communicate what it wanted the living to know.

The spirit of a man came through for a woman who had remarried after her first husband had died. He wanted to seek her forgiveness for some past offense, but the woman refused and told him to "go away." The spirit of a mother, who had been dead for forty years, reached out for her daughter. The mother wanted her daughter to know that she had been present throughout all the difficult times her daughter had experienced during all those years.

At a séance, a spirit can also come through a participant other than Jane. One man had recently lost his niece to multiple sclerosis. Directly opposite him another man became possessed by the girl's spirit and could not stand up. To release the girl's spirit, two strong men had to hold the man up while Jane called the spirit out.

Fascinated with the psychic events of the evening and the charm of Olde Stone Cottage, several guests asked me to relate any historical events that may have happened here, or to which the residents of Cutter Farm may have been witness. Eager to oblige, I described the events that follow.

The first account involved John Adams. In August of 1774, he made his first trip out of New England to attend the First Continental Congress in Philadelphia. As his New England delegation traveled through Woodbridge, militia and townspeople turned out to greet them. After a likely stop at the Cross Keys Tavern there, Adams traveled west on the King's Highway. He no doubt went right past the Cutter Farm, where we were all gathered, and then continued on to New Brunswick, Princeton, and finally Trenton, to board a ferry for Philadelphia.

Again, with the April 19, 1775 news of Lexington and Concord and the thunder of the bombardment of Bunker Hill left behind him, John Adams departed his home in Braintree, Massachusetts in January 1776 for a Second Continental Congress in Philadelphia. As British General Sir William Howe's twenty regiments of Redcoats occupied Boston, Adams' delegation would have stopped several times a day to eat, sleep, or tend their horses in New Jersey's taverns and residences.

The second event, which occurred when the British invaded New Jersey, is long shrouded in the darkness of the past. The "Long Retreat"–from Fort Lee to the crossing of the Delaware to final safety at Trenton– occurred between November 20 and December 7, 1776. Traveling down the King's Highway, Commander-in-Chief General George Washington, Artillery Captain Alexander Hamilton, Lieutenant James Monroe and approximately 3,000 poorly equipped, thinly clad and hungry Continental soldiers passed by the Cutter Farm early in the morning hours of November 29, 1776. In pursuit were 6,000 vigilant, well-equipped and professionally trained Redcoat and Hessian mercenary forces under the leadership of Major General Lord Charles Cornwallis. Tom Paine, limping along with the Continentals while scribbling at every stop, would eventually finish writing the famous words that were to become a series of pamphlets entitled "The American Crisis."

Paine, an impoverished Englishman who had been raised a Quaker, had no formal education and no consistent career, and certainly no love for the English Crown. After King George III had declared the colonies to be in a state of rebellion, he volunteered to serve as a civilian aide on General Nathanael Greene's staff, and wrote a series of pamphlets. The most famous was "Common Sense," which lambasted the tyranny of the king and unequivocally endorsed independence. It was unquestionably the most influential and notorious pamphlet of the American Revolution. In it, he deconstructed the idea that freedom could coexist with monarchy, asserting that "The Law is King", i.e., a nation governed by law. It sold more than 100,000 copies within weeks of its January 1776 publication, and became the most widely read piece of literature published in America.

The third event occurred long after the 1783 Treaty of Paris, which effectively ended the American Revolutionary War. On April 16, 1789, George Washington began a journey by coach from his home at Mount Vernon, Virginia, to his inauguration as the first President of the United States of America in New York City. On April 22, after an overnight stay in Princeton, while en route to the Cross Keys Tavern in Woodbridge, his carriage and entourage passed by the Cutter Farm. All along his route up the King's Highway, "Farmers assembled at crossroads, gentry bowed dignified welcome from their porches and wayside inns, and soldiers who had fought their nation's battles saluted and cheered."

Olde Stone Cottage at Cutter Farm, with its rolling lawns, gardens, extensive grounds and remaining outbuildings, is being carefully preserved for future generations. It remains in private ownership.

The Battle of Monmouth

t was a hot, muggy June day, the first day of summer. Jane was ready when I called for her at two o'clock in the afternoon. Our drive was to take us through portions of Middlesex, Somerset, Hunterdon, and Monmouth counties, along roads traversing the Raritan and Millstone River valleys and their offshoots.

One of my favorite roads in New Jersey is old Route 514. The Dutch laid out this road in 1655, after Governor Petrus Stuyvesant had gained control over Nieuw Netherland in 1647. Roughly paralleling a major Lenni Lenape Indian trail, it began at *Nieuw Amsterdam*, crossed the bay via ferry to a point near Elizabeth, and spanned the areas that would become Woodbridge and Piscataway (near present day Edison), ending at the ford of the Raritan River (the ford became Inian's Ferry in 1681).

Later, in 1724, Inian's Ferry was renamed New Brunswick in honor of the ascension of the House of Brunswick (a German duchy of the House of Hanover) to the throne of Great Britain in the person of King George I. Continuing from New Brunswick, Route 514 becomes Amwell Road in Franklin Township, (a name it has proudly borne for more than 200 years, in honor of the last Royal Governor of New Jersey.)

Jane and I took Amwell Road from New Brunswick to East Millstone, passing by the old Franklin Inn, built circa 1752. The home of Cornelius and Anje Van Liew, thos is where General Lord Charles Cornwallis is said to have stayed during the Second Middlebush Encampment in 1778-79.

The adjacent Six Mile Run Historic District on South Middlebush Road, Franklin Township, features exceptionally well-preserved vistas of the Dutch-

One of the locks along the Delaware & Raritan Canal. Now a park, it provides a pleasant place for strolls, biking and boating.

General Lord Charles Cornwallis is believed to have spent the Second Middlebush Encampment of 1778-1779 at the Franklin Inn. Many assume that Franklin Township was named after Benjamin Franklin. In fact, it honors his Loyalist son, William, the last Royal Governor of New Jersey.

settled rural nineteenth century landscape that once characterized the entire Raritan Valley. Contributing structures include numerous farmsteads, Dutch and English barns, smoke houses, corncribs, granaries and many related outbuildings.

The Delaware & Raritan Canal, completed in 1834, was one of America's greatest inland waterways. Excavated in the valleys of the three rivers it connects–the Raritan, the Millstone, and the Delaware–it was an engineering marvel that ran south through Central New Jersey to New Brunswick, finally emptying into the Raritan River. During its peak years of 1866-1871, it carried more freight than any other canal in America. Closed in 1933, it was declared a state park in 1974. As we watched canoes paddling on the canal, Jane commented, "What a lovely way to spend a Sunday afternoon!"

Crossing the 44-mile-long Delaware and Raritan Canal and the 38-mile-long Millstone River, we continued west to Ringoes, where Amwell Road terminates. We then followed Route 179 south to Lambertville (Coryell's Ferry). It was here that Commander-in-Chief General George Washington and his troops entered New Jersey on June 20, 1778, after having left their encampment at Valley Forge in Pennsylvania.

Driving east from Lambertville on Route 518, we then followed the same route Washington and his Continental Army took for their rendezvous with the British Army at Monmouth Court House (present day Freehold, New Jersey).

Our first stop was at Hopewell Borough, where on June 23, 1778, the Continental Army encamped on the farm of John Hart, one of New Jersey's five signers of the Declaration of Independence. The nearby Hunt House, built of stone and timber in 1752, was the farmstead of the Joseph Stouts family (he was a descendant of Penelope Van Princis Stout, who was shipwrecked on Sandy Hook, New Jersey in 1620).

Hunt House is in the shadow of the red shale Sourland Mountain. It was here that Washington held his celebrated council of war, attended by the greatest single assemblage of American officers, proposing the action that would result in the Battle of Monmouth.

At Hopewell, Washington ordered an advance guard of four thousand men under Major General Marie-Joseph du Motier, the Marquis de Lafayette, to proceed eight miles to the east of Kingston. This maneuver was intended to place these troops directly in line with Sir Henry Clinton's route toward New Brunswick and Perth Amboy, should Clinton proceed in a northerly direction.

Major General Charles Lee, second in command, "who preferred to let the British force parade unmolested across the State," looked that day "anxious and indignant that his military experience and judgment" had not persuaded his associates– Washington, Greene, Hamilton, Stirling, Lafayette, von Steuben, Knox, Poor, Wayne, Woodford, Patterson,

The Marquis de Lafayette and George Washington during the bitterly cold days at Valley Forge.

The bas-relief of the Council of War as it appears on the Battle of Monmouth monument.

Scott, Scammel, and Duportail.

Lee's anxious look is well illustrated on one of the bas-relief images on the Battle of Monmouth Monument at Freehold, which depicts the outstanding leaders of the Revolution seated around the council of war table at Hopewell during a total solar eclipse on June 24, 1778. General Washington is listening attentively while Lafayette urges immediate action, with Von Steuben and Duportail apparently in agreement. Patterson and Greene would force an engagement too. Colonel Alexander Scammel, Adjutant-General, who was later to die at Yorktown, is shown busily engaged recording the opinions of the experts and hoping that General Wayne, who wants to say something equally forceful, will wait until Lafayette is finished. Only Lee is sitting back, scoffing, and grumbling under his breath. It was during this meeting that it was decided to skip a direct attack on the twelve-mile-long British baggage train, and alternately attack its rear guard and seize a part of it.

I then told Jane that General Sir William Howe's forces had invaded the "rebel capital" of Philadelphia on September 26, 1777, via the Chesapeake Bay, after successfully engaging the Americans at Brandywine, Delaware on September 11, 1777 and again on October 4, 1777 at Germantown, Pennsylvania. British General John Burgoyne, without General Howe's troops, was en route from Canada, but they were badly defeated by American General Horatio Gates at Saratoga on October 17, 1777. As a result of Gates's victory and the diplomacy of the celebrated Benjamin Franklin, America's most distinguished citizen in Europe, France was at last willing to consider an alliance with America. The two countries signed treaties in February 1778, and France entered the war, boosting the confidence of the patriot cause. "I've always admired Ben Franklin," Jane said.

While General Howe and his regiments led a life of comfort in Philadelphia during the winter of 1777-78,

Washington would comment from Valley Forge about his ragged army, saying, "we had in camp not less than 2,898 men unfit for duty by reason of their being barefoot and other-wise naked." The camp was pitched in the middle of a rich and fertile county, but the farmers chose to trade their produce to the British, rather than to the Continentals in exchange for worthless money. At Valley Forge, Prussian volunteer Baron Friedrich Wilhelm von Steuben proceeded to teach the new army how to march and maneuver, and improved sanitary conditions throughout the camp. The Americans also learned how to use bayonets effectively, a skill that would come in handy in several upcoming battles.

Sir Henry Clinton

The French recognition of the Revolutionary regime in February 1778, followed by Spain and Holland, threatened the British naval supply route to Philadelphia. In the spring of 1778, Sir Henry Clinton, had replaced Sir William Howe, and had been ordered to take the British army back to New York. Under the threat of a possible French blockade of Delaware Bay, Clinton chose to march his 20,000 British troops directly across New Jersey to New York.

A rare picture of Strawberry Hill, the West Jersey plantation of Royal Governor William Franklin.

Crossing the Delaware River at Cooper's Ferry (now Camden), the twelve-mile-long baggage train of the Royal Army traveled by way of Gloucester, Haddonfield and Mount Holly (not far from Rancocas and "Strawberry Hill," (not to be confused with Strawberry Hill in Woodbridge) the former 600-acre West Jersey plantation of Royal Governor William Franklin). Mount Holly is where Prince William Henry, Duke of Clarence, later King William IV of Great Britain, had been stationed with British troops. The army then continued on to Crosswicks, Allentown, Clarksburg, and eventually Freehold.

By now, Washington's forces had been reinforced by fresh enlistments of patriots who had been heartened by the successes of Trenton, Princeton, and above all, Saratoga, as well as the consequent French entry into

The Cranbury Inn

the war. The American army numbered about 14,500, including about 1,000 militia. The British army numbered about 21,000, including 4,100 Hessians, 2,100 Loyalists, with an additional 1,000 women and children in tow.

As we followed in Washington's footsteps, we continued east on Route 518, crossing Province Line Road, which separates Hunterdon and Somerset counties. This line is the original division line between East and West Jersey. The Rev. George Keith of Perth Amboy, Surveyor General of East Jersey, was the first to survey the line, in 1687. Continuing on present Route 518, we followed Washington's route through Rocky Hill to Kingston and then on to Cranbury.

Benjamin Franklin, as a boy of seventeen, had taken the ferry from Perth Amboy to South Amboy and walked across New Jersey to Burlington en route to Philadelphia on what was known as the Federal Road. Since the road passed through Cranbury, an important stagecoach stop was at the Cranbury Inn. It was on June 26, 1778, that Washington arrived at Cranbury, unable to advance the army any further because of intense summer heat and pelting rain. While the soldiers camped in the Cranbury area, Washington made his headquarters at the home of Dr. Hezekiah Stites, on South Main Street. Here he met with Lafayette, Hamilton, and other officers.

Our visit to Cranbury included a brief stop at the burying ground behind the Presbyterian Church, which, as a psychic, Jane found very intriguing. Repositories of history, graveyards also contain memorable and fascinating epitaphs. Early poets seem to have had a field day preparing rhymes and embellishing written memorials, agreeing or disagreeing with the grimacing skulls or the pouting, periwigged angels above them. Perhaps the most dismal inscription of the lot is that chosen for Humphrey Mount, an elder of the Presbyterian congregation, who is buried under a stone brought from Woodbridge:

> "From this cold bed of humid clay
>   Reader to you I cry:
> Your time is short, make no delay,
>   Prepare, prepare to die."

Departing Cranbury, we then followed the narrow road George Washington and the Continentals took on June 27 as they crossed ten miles of rolling farmland, woods and marshes to the high ground of Gravel Hill. This placed them just west of Manalapan Brook near the Matchaponix River in present Monroe Township. On that day in 1778, there were loud claps of thunder in the air, and the excessive heat (100 degrees plus) and humidity caused many Americans to perish from heat prostration and sunstroke. The victims were buried along the road through Monroe Township, and near their encampment at Gravel Hill, on the evening before the Battle of Monmouth. Included among the survivors was James Monroe, the fifth President of the United States. George Washington made his headquarters that evening at the house of John Anderson, just outside Gravel Hill.

On June 26, 1778, the British forces camped west of Monmouth Court House alongside the Allentown Road, with heavy rain and thunder continuing all night. The next day General Clinton learned that enemy forces were operating around his preferred route via New Brunswick to New York City. He changed his plans and elected to go the Sandy Hook route. The night of June 27 brought even more heat and heavy thunder, perhaps foreshadowing upcoming events.

Sunday, June 28, dawned a brutally hot and humid day, with temperatures soaring close to 100 degrees. Within a fifteen mile span, the Battle of Monmouth was to occur on this day in the nearby hills, meadows, hedgerows, and marshy ravines drained by the

Emanuel Gottlieb Leutze, who created the iconic painting of Washington crossing the Delaware River, also created this image of the General rallying his troops at the Battle of Monmouth.

Spotwood North, Middle and South Brooks. This area was located between Old Tennent Church and the broader land surrounding Monmouth Court House (Freehold).

Monmouth Battlefield State Park, situated on 1,813 acres in Manalapan, commemorates this battle, the largest major land offensive of the American forces in terms of the number of troops engaged. It was also the fiercest artillery battle of the Revolution, and the longest one-day engagement of the war.

The Battle of Monmouth, the hardest fought engagement of the American Revolution, was a "pell-mell" contest between regiments and detachments, as opposed to brigades and divisions. Even today, after much consideration, it is difficult to be certain of the exact sequence and timing of events.

Further confusion was added by Major General Charles Lee, who had been recently released by the British after his incarceration between December 1776-

May 1778 in a prisoner exchange. Considering an American victory unlikely, he favored a negotiated peace, and may have been influenced by his soft treatment while a captive. Overcome by Clinton's superior forces, he was forced to retreat, causing Washington to conclude Lee had not obeyed his orders to attack. Washington met the retreating troops and assumed command, desperately seeking to reorganize them.

General Charles Lee fought his court martial by publicly attacking George Washington's character.

Long hours of struggle ensued, under the baking sun, until Clinton finally ordered a withdrawal that evening. Washington directed his energy-sapped men to sleep on the ground they occupied, with their firearms close at hand, to await the next day's events. However, as soon as it was dark, Clinton's army rapidly and silently slipped away, leaving Washington to conclude that pursuit was pointless.

On June 29 Washington and his troops returned to Englishtown. Here, at the Village Inn, he issued orders to commence the court martial that General Charles Lee had asked for "to clear his good name." The inquiry, presided over by Lord Stirling, lasted six weeks, with the court moving with the army. General Lee was charged with disobedience of orders, misbehavior before the army, and disrespect towards the Commander-in-Chief. Lafayette, General and Wayne were among the twenty-six witnesses who testified against him; Henry Knox headed the smaller number that appeared in his defense.

Jane Doherty, using her remarkable gift as a paranormal investigator, visited the battlefield and further corroborated battle events as she "heard" the blood-curdling screams of soldiers charging and the noise of cannons firing at extremely close range. With Jane's impressions of gravesites and mass burials, she was able to pinpoint the spot where she believes bodies are buried.

In the Belleterre section, Jane felt heavy troop movement crossing the road. At the Hedgerow, where the Americans had drawn the British into the open field, Jane sensed the intense battle that had taken place there. And in an area where campfires had been lit after the battle, Jane described a vision of people huddled around an open campfire with a kettle positioned over it. At this very same location, a kettle had been unearthed.

Hundreds of men fell victim to the brutal sun, a factor that helped to create the American legend of Molly Pitcher. Mary Hays, known as Molly, followed her husband into battle carrying pitchers of water dipped from Perrine's Spring to thirsty soldiers. Tradition says that when her husband was wounded, Molly stepped up to replace him at his cannon.

The legend of Molly Pitcher was based on Mary Hays, who was said to bring pitchers of water to thirsty men and then gamely stepped in to replace her wounded husband at the cannon. The incident was celebrated with this Currier & Ives print.

Old Tennent Church, erected in 1751, and situated three miles southeast of Englishtown and three miles west of Freehold, was founded by Scottish political and religious Dissenters. The Battle of Monmouth raged around the church, and it was used as a field hospital to house wounded American soldiers. Because of its rich history and magnificent beauty, it regularly appears in leading surveys of American architecture. Its ministers were ardent supporters of the Revolution, and because of this affiliation, it is a shrine to freedom. Jane admired the beauty of its architecture. It replaced the much earlier Old Scots Meeting House, in Topenamus, Marlboro Township, built in 1692. Old Scots was constructed at the site where its pastor, the first Presbyterian minister in America, John Boyd, was ordained on May 29, 1706. He died two years later on August 30,

1708, and his is the oldest grave in the adjacent cemetery.

Samuel Craig, who built Craig House in 1746, (scene of heavy fighting on Monmouth Battlefield) is buried at Old Scots Churchyard, several miles from Old Tennent, along with other early Scottish settlers. In 1778, John Craig, paymaster of the American Army, owned this house. His family had fled after casting the family silver into the adjacent well for hiding. The restored house has huge fireplaces, hand hewn ceiling beams, a paneled hall and stairway reminiscent of Old Tennent Church. The house was also used as a field hospital by both sides.

The Craig House was witness to heavy fighting during the Battle of Monmouth and is now in need of restoration.

The tombstones in Old Tennent's graveyard on White Oak Hill, and in the fields beyond the church, mark not only refugees from political persecution in Scotland. They also denote the final resting places of blue-clad patriot Continentals and British Redcoats of the king, both lying side by side.

The Battle of Monmouth was a political and psychological triumph for the Continental Army and for Washington. It marked a turning point in the war. Washington had proved himself as a field marshal, and the British were on the defensive. The American forces, which had profited from the drill and discipline they had received under General von Steuben's tutelage at Valley Forge, proved themselves capable of holding their own against veteran British troops in open field battle.

Nonetheless, many men were unnecessarily lost. Clinton suffered 1,200 casualties–including those wounded, killed, and captured–to Washington's 300-400. Clinton's march was not delayed to a great extent, nor had any part of his baggage train been captured. Late in the evening, Clinton had resumed his travel down Dutch Lane Road through Colts Neck, Holmdel, Middletown, and across the Navesink Hills to Sandy Hook.

While en route, a number of small skirmishes were

Buried where he fell in 1778, private Michael Field's grave is at least marked, unlike many who were killed.

fought with the soldiers that guarded Clinton's retreating baggage train. The location of the marked grave of Michael Field, a private in the First Regiment of New Jersey Militia from Somerset County, is no different from the location of thousands of other soldiers who died in the Revolution, although many are buried in unmarked graves. His remains lie forever on the spot where he died on June 28, 1778, during one of these skirmishes. His grave is still preserved on Heyers Mill Road in Colts Neck. In terms of lives lost, the American Revolution was the second most costly war in American history.

Looking back for one last glance at the battlefield landscape that we had just crossed, we reflected on the hours of painful confrontation and overwhelming anxiety that had occurred there. Jane and I paused together in the privacy of silence, contemplating all that we had experienced. These moments that we savored were further enhanced as we invited the quietness of solitude to be our guest. Finally, Jane quietly remarked, "This battlefield, like much of life, is spiritually unexplored country."

The final leg of our afternoon drive took us north by way of Englishtown to Spotswood, named after Spotteswoode, in Ochiltree, Scotland, the ancestral estate of Doctor John Johnstone of Perth Amboy and his brother James, both of whom were Proprietors of East Jersey. Their total land holdings in this area numbered some 15,000 acres. The Americans camped at Spotswood on July 1, 1778, before continuing their journey the next day toward New Brunswick.

New Brunswick citizens cheered hoarsely when Washington and his men marched into town. Washington offered his weary troops a time for rest and relaxation, establishing a camp along present-day George Street and in the open fields of Raritan Landing near the site of present-day Johnson Park, on River Road, Piscataway until July 7, 1778. Washington and his staff stayed at Ross Hall, the commodious and elegant residence of the widow Sara Ross, the wife of a medical doctor who had died three years previously. The home was situated on a 350-acre farm estate in Piscataway, not far from Metlar's Lane and the Metlar-Bodine House (circa 1728 and one of two lone survivors of the earlier village of Raritan Landing).

The Metlar-Bodine House represents one of the last vestiges of the 18th century Raritan Landing community.

It was from Ross Hall that Washington, on July 3, 1778, issued an order for his 12,000 troops to line the New Brunswick waterfront on the following afternoon for the highlight of their bivouac—a wave-like firing of their muskets in salute to the second anniversary of our national independence. Celebrated with a Grand Review, this was the first official observance of the 4th of July. Soldiers and citizens alike would not soon forget that glorious day. "I had no idea that the 4th of July was first observed right here in New Jersey. How amazing!" Jane said.

On the evening of July Fourth, after the military exercise, Washington invited his officers, including the Marquis de Lafayette, Alexander Hamilton, James McHenry, Baron von Steuben, and Nathanael Greene, and their ladies back to headquarters—Ross Hall—for a ball to mark the national independence holiday.

By July 5, British transports had evacuated Clinton's forces from Sandy Hook back to New York City. In the meantime, all Britain (including their sovereign King George III) could do was to strategize how they might successfully end the war while maintaining their proverbial British stiff upper lip.

Part Four

Headquarters & Generals

The Wallace House

Somerville, New Jersey

During the Second Middlebrook Encampment, between December 11, 1778 and June 3, 1779, General Washington leased the Wallace House for his headquarters. The encampment at Middlebrook is the least known of the Revolutionary War campaigns in New Jersey. However, it was crucial to the outcome of the American Revolution. Washington chose the area because it was easily defensible, had a good network of roads, plenty of timber for the soldiers' huts, and a sympathetic populace nearby. Compared to the winters spent at Valley Forge, Pennsylvania, or Morristown, New Jersey, the winter of 1779 was mild, and the army was better fed, clothed and trained. While Washington's strategy was to convince the British not to move again into New Jersey, or advance north into New England, he was now better prepared to engage them if they decided to do so.

Following the Battle of Monmouth, Washington anticipated that the next major thrust by the British from their New York stronghold would be northward. In an effort to repulse their advance, in November 1778 he positioned his army in a series of camps that crossed halfway around New York City and its environs. This arrangement allowed Washington to detect and respond to any British forays toward Philadelphia, Albany, or New England, while keeping him poised for a joint attack with the French on New York City.

There were several British forays into war-torn New Jersey, but Sir Henry Clinton did not attempt any decisive action. Clinton would later determine Middlebrook too strong, and Washington's 10,000 troops too numerous, to

The hard-drinking and hard-driving William Alexander assumed the title of "Lord Stirling" and was the only man of such distinction to side with the Americans as a general.

be "rashly attempted" with his force of 22,000 soldiers from the New York and Rhode Island areas.

The Continental Army, consisting of about 10,000 men, was equal to the entire population of Somerset County. To minimize its impact on the population, the brigades were assigned to locations several miles apart: "Maryland" to the east of Middlebrook, "Virginia" on the west, "Pennsylvania" across the Raritan on the west side of the Millstone River and in the Artillery Camp at Pluckemin.

Other encampments were garrisoned along a 75-mile-long line from Middlebrook, toward Summit, Ramapo, and West Point. Others stretched from Fishkill to Danbury in Western Connecticut. Under orders from Washington dated April 12, 1779, a series of twenty-three bonfire signal-beacons were built to warn the American militia to arms in the event of any advance by the British troops. Each beacon was constructed of logs in the shape of a pyramid. The New Jersey Militia constructed stations nine through twenty-three. When set ablaze, they became a huge and noticeable flare. "What a smart idea," Jane said.

These orders were carried out under the leadership of Major General William Alexander, of Basking Ridge in Somerset County. Commonly known as "Lord Stirling," he claimed his title as a Scottish Earl through his father. Although the claim was somewhat questionable, he was the only man of such distinction to become an American general. George Washington referred to him as "my Lord," and thought well of the fifty-six-year-old, wealthy, hard-driving and hard-drinking patriot. He had led his small force at the Battle of Long Island with extraordinary valor.

John Wallace, a wealthy fabric importer and merchant from Philadelphia, had an eight-room addition, constructed between 1775 and 1776, added on to an earlier small farmhouse. Today, it is one of the finest and most original examples of Georgian architecture in New Jersey and was one of the largest

houses constructed in the state during the Revolution.

In the eighteenth century, the Dutch-framed mansion fronted the Old York Road, one of the main highways across New Jersey, connecting New York and Philadelphia. Washington chose the Wallace House because of its strategic location and amenities. Other generals and their aides were quartered in the homes of nearby residents. The Wallace House became a New Jersey State historic site in 1947. Washington spent six months there, excepting a six-week trip to Philadelphia, undertaken to address Congress. Martha Washington, as was her custom, joined her husband on February 5, 1779 after his return to Wallace House, and stayed there throughout the spring.

The Washingtons ordered a new set of china and "six tolerably genteel but not expensive candle-sticks" through the assistant quartermaster at Philadelphia. They enjoyed gracious entertaining, and "Lady Kitty" Livingston and her sister, Mrs. John Jay, were their frequent guests. Other distinguished visitors included

Washington really did sleep at the Wallace House!

Colonel Henry Rutgers,
Revolutionary war hero
and philanthropist, was
an early benefactor of
Rutgers University.

The Old Dutch Parsonage

the Marquis de Lafayette, Baron von Steuben, Lt. Col. Alexander Hamilton, General Washington's aide-de-camp, and Major General Benedict Arnold. The Washingtons also socialized with prominent citizens in the area, including the Reverend Jacob R. Hardenburg, Pastor of the local Dutch Reformed Church.

The Reverend Hardenburg had sold the farmstead, "Hope Farm," of 107 acres near his parsonage, (built of Holland brick for the Reverend John Frelinghuysen) to John Wallace in 1775 in anticipation of building a summer residence in the tranquility of Somerset County. Hardenburg was a strong supporter of independence and was instrumental in the founding of Queen's College, serving as its first president from 1785-1790. The theological classes held at Old Dutch Parsonage were the beginning of the college, later to become Rutgers University. "Isn't it interesting to learn how things get started," Jane said.

The Great Awakening of the mid-eighteenth century, religious in nature, promoting the freedoms of man in a civil society and the possibilities of what free men could do, found a home in two major educational institutions of eighteenth century New Jersey–the College of New Jersey (later named Princeton University) and Queen's College.

Historically, Rutgers was the eighth college established in the American colonies. After it had been chartered in 1766, it was named for the consort of Britain's King George III. The college was renamed in 1825 in honor of Colonel Henry Rutgers, a benefactor and Revolutionary War veteran. It officially became Rutgers, the State University, in 1945.

Sometimes, at the end of the day, when a low sun is streaming through the panes of the window in what was Washington's small library, one can visualize the shadowy figure of Major Caleb Gibbs. He was the commandant of the Life Guard, an elite corps of about 144 men who served as the equivalent of Washington's secret service, closely guarding him, his staff, and his papers. Jane sensed Gibbs' presence, as have others before her.

It was at Wallace House that George Washington planned the successful Indian Campaign of 1779 against the Iroquois League, fierce allies of the British. With the war in the colonies at something of a standstill, Washington decided to dispatch troops to northern Pennsylvania and western New York State, where the Iroquois Indians' Six Nations Confederation and Loyalist forces were attacking American frontier towns and outposts.

Major General John Sullivan's forces of about 4,000 Continental Army troops drove the Iroquois to Fort Niagara, the British stronghold. This allowed the American colonists to push westward and populate the region that lay out before them.

The winter and spring of 1779 passed quietly. The weather was mild and fine; the spirits of the troops were excellent. Except for endemic fighting along the Hackensack River in Bergen County, there was little military movement in New Jersey or elsewhere to the north.

Threats of an enemy attack on West Point pulled the Americans out of Middlebrook on June 3, 1779, for a forced march to the Hudson River, but the attack never came. With Washington absent from New Jersey, Colonel John Graves Simcoe, Commander of Clinton's elite Queen's Rangers, staged a terrifying raid in October 1779, pounding through the Raritan

John Graves Simcoe served the crown as the first Lieutenant Governor of Upper Canada before commanding a contingent of Rangers that terrorized the Raritan and Millstone Valleys.

and Millstone Valleys in a dash that many historians have labeled the most daring single event of the war. He and his Rangers covered fifty-five miles in a single night. Simcoe was captured, but most of the Rangers made it to safety. Jane could feel the terror the Rangers had inflicted on the citizenry.

With the close of an uneventful 1779 summer campaign, Washington again selected Morristown, New Jersey as the site for his winter encampment. From its heights, he could keep a watchful eye on the British in New York City, and be in a position to move his soldiers over well-guarded routes to either the Hudson or the Delaware. The several divisions of his army constructed log huts in Jockey Hollow, three miles southwest of town, while Washington and his official family occupied the Ford Mansion on the outskirts of Morristown. The winter was the most severe since 1755, and much worse than that of 1778 at Valley Forge. The prospect of ultimate victory seemed distant.

The Van Veighten House

*I*t was May Day, and the dogwood, cherry blossoms and tulips–red and butter yellow–were in full bloom. The scent of lilac and hyacinth, too, were in the air. Spring had come rushing in all uninvited, riotous, loud, overwhelming, and lush. The tree leaves had started budding out, hinting at the verdure that was to come. Moreover, we were on our way to the Van Veighten House.

There are a total of five houses preserved as historic sites in Somerset County that had been used as headquarters during the Second Middlebrook Encampment. Besides the Van Veighten House, the others are the Wallace House (General Washington), the Van Horne House (General Alexander, Lord Stirling), the Abraham Staats House (Baron von Steuben), and the Jacobus Vanderveer House (General Henry Knox). Of the five, the Van Veighten House proved by far to be the most ominous.

During the Second Middlebrook Encampment, the house served as headquarters for Quartermaster General Nathanael Greene. Built in 1722 with bricks imported from Holland, it was later remodeled, in 1840, in a Dutch vernacular style.

Jane and I had become more determined to visit Van Veighten House, after weeks of trying to obtain access. From Finderne Avenue (Route 533), we drove down Van Veighten Road as far as we could go. The road seemed to possess an aura that put us in touch with our most deeply rooted fears. It seemed like a passageway into the unknown, a conduit to the out of the ordinary and an inlet into the isolated shadowy past. We both felt uneasy and uncomfortable.

A thought unwillingly crept into my mind, as if some tombstone carver had chiseled it there. All that was missing from this scene were signs saying "Keep Out," "Go Away," and "Not Responsible For Injury Or Death." That is how uninviting the place seemed.

General Nathanael Greene was thirty-seven when he arrived at the Van Veighten House. Born in Rhode Island into a Quaker family, he knew little of military life. Beyond his basic training in the local militia, everything Greene knew about strategy and warfare he had taught himself, by reading from his extensive library of more than 200 books. Since he had grown up in the family's foundry business, hammering iron ship anchors and chains, he had far less formal education that some of his genteel counterparts in the Continental Army. However, he had received some tutoring in Latin and mathematics at home, and had been encouraged by Reverend Ezra Stiles, later President of Yale University.

Handsome and good-natured, Greene was caught up in the general fervor of resistance in New England, as relations between England and the thirteen North American colonies deteriorated. He had renounced the Friends' (Quaker) philosophy of nonviolence and was expelled from his congregation in 1773. He joined the local militia in that year in order to aid in resisting British policies.

Somewhat overweight, Greene walked with a limp and had one eye that was clouded from a bout with smallpox. Despite appearances, his calm demeanor inspired confidence in all those around him, and politics soon offered him a better path. He was elected to the Rhode Island Legislature, and then

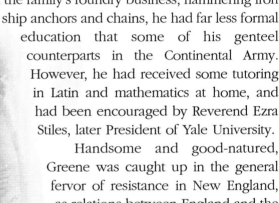

General Nathaneal Greene, taken from a Charles Willson Peale portrait.

appointed Brigadier General of the state's "Army of Observation," which he led to Boston. There he met George Washington. Within a year Washington would consider Greene the best of his generals, suitable to succeed him in case of his death or capture.

Serving in the Battles of Long Island, Harlem Heights and Fort Lee in 1776, he was promoted to the rank of major general. He played a prominent role in the Battles of Trenton, Princeton, Brandywine and Germantown. On March 2, 1778, Washington appointed Greene the new Quartermaster General of the Continental Army. Later, in the campaign in the South that set the stage for the last major battle, at Yorktown, Greene would prove himself the most brilliant American field commander of the war.

He took an active role in three New Jersey battles: the Battle of Monmouth, on June 28, 1778; the engagement at Connecticut Farms on June 7, 1780, where he commanded the front line; and the Second Battle of Springfield on June 23, 1780, (often referred to as the "forgotten victory") in which he led the force that repulsed the British and caused them to retreat from New Jersey for the last time. However, it was during the winter and spring of 1779 that Greene found himself with Washington's forces in the heavily Netherland Dutch county of Somerset, New Jersey, where Dutch was the dominant language.

The Dutch phase of New Jersey history roughly dates from 1621 to 1664, with hubs of Dutch settlement in Bergen, Middlesex, Monmouth and Somerset counties. These communities were parts of the *Nieuw Nederland* Dutch Colony in North America, whose capital was *Nieuw Amsterdam* from 1613-64, (present day Manhattan). In 1776, a patchwork of different accents and languages could be heard in these counties. "I had no idea," Jane commented.

English Puritans had arrived in New Jersey after 1664 from Long Island and Connecticut. Although the English outnumbered any other single group, other

The strong influence of the Dutch in colonial New Jersey dates back to the New Netherlands settlement at what is today New York. This skyline view was created by Johannes Vingsboons in 1664.

nationalities were well represented.

Although English and Dutch were the dominant languages in New Jersey, there were also French and Germans, from the Palatinate of the Rhine, and Scots, such as the Ulster Scots (the so-called Scots-Irish) who were ethnically Scottish. While English was the common tongue in the area, many residents spoke the language with the very thick accent of their countries of origin.

The African American population spoke the language of their masters, but some of their own unique languages survived in expressions and idioms. "From this promiscuous breed," observed a French settler, "that race now called Americans has arisen."

Prior to the American Revolution, there were approximately three million residents in the colonies, but only one tenth lived in large towns or cities. Philadelphia had nearly 25,000 people, and New York had about 20,000. The population of New Jersey, by the end of the American Revolution, was around 150,000, with slightly fewer than 10 percent being slaves or Free Blacks. "How so few people could do so much for the cause of independence is really incredible," Jane said.

There were tensions among the Jersey Dutch factions of patriots and Loyalists regarding the subject of the colonies' proper relationship to England's king. Dutch ideas traditionally associated with the Netherlands (tolerance, freedom of conscience, economic justice and civil concord) have left us a legacy that goes beyond the Dutch houses and barns. Dutch tolerance, however, did not extend to slaves.

By 1737, New Jersey had one slave for every twelve

people; Somerset County in particular had a slave population of fifteen percent. Dutch farmers typically used African slaves, although slaves from other locales were also common. In Perth Amboy, nearly every house "swarmed with African slaves." It was in Perth Amboy where the Royal African Company established a major slave center, transporting shiploads of misery to America. As for discipline, it was at the whim of the owner, and the ultimate punishment of burning at the stake was not unheard of. At Perth Amboy, in 1729, an African man named Prince, charged with the murder of William Cook, was burned in such a manner. "How terrible," Jane exclaimed.

Among the Northern Colonies, New Jersey and New York had the largest population of slaves. Despite the Continental Congress's 1775 decision to exclude Africans, both slave and free, from the Continental Army, New Jersey's Militia Act of 1777 allowed the enlistment of Free Blacks.

As Jane and I entered General Greene's Headquarters, our hostess greeted us with a rather

Perth Amboy was a major port for the importation of slaves from Africa. Along with Delaware, New Jersey would be the last of the northern states states to ratify the 13th Amendment to the Constitution outlawing slavery.

Once home to General Greene and his wife, who hosted a party where Washington danced the night away, the Van Veighten house now collects dust...and perhaps some ghosts.

grave yet thoughtful expression on her face. She had just seen the blurry figure of a person in grayish white, with no distinctive facial features, descend the creaking and carpetless main staircase. Evidently, this shadowy figure, a constant resident, vanished too suddenly to be definable. All the same, our hostess told us that there was something dark and sinister about the occurrence.

Once inside, we began our tour by quietly ascending this same staircase, conscious that only some disembodied listener could hear us. The second floor is a maze of rooms, but after a few false starts we reached the bedroom where General and Mrs. Greene stayed.

It was a cheerless and dusty room, which had been untenanted so long–except by spiders, mice, and ghosts–that it was overgrown with desolation. No doubt, it had been a room of great and varied human experiences, with many scenes from past lives acted out there. Its walls knew the joy of bridal nights, the agony and relief of a bedchamber where new immortals had first drawn earthly breath, and the sadness and dread of the old and infirm as they spent their last seconds on Earth.

Ghosts sometimes produce odors, Jane explained, leaving "a perfume scent, a tobacco scent or whiskey scent, for example, as paranormal proof of their need to get our attention." With an anxious heart, I now listened as Jane described the slowly pacing footsteps of this menacing resident, now in spirit, moving across its chosen path in this very room, leaving a foul odor in its wake. Returned from the dead from some old family mausoleum, we could literally smell a stench like some rotting corpse. Like death, but without death's quiet privilege–its freedom from all mortal care–we quickly slipped away to the first floor. To this day, no one knows the identity of this spectral resident.

Once back downstairs, we entered the large formal

parlor. Here at a "pretty little frisk," in mid-March, 1779, George Washington was observed to have danced with Mrs. Greene "upwards of three hours without once sitting down," in a rare (and probably more traditional than true) show of endurance. Washington had learned to dance at a young age– Virginians loved to dance and he was no exception.

General Greene had possessed a slight limp from childhood. This, combined with his admiration and respect for Washington, certainly makes his willingness to allow Washington to dance so long with his wife, Katherine, (Caty) plausible. Greene had named his first son, born in 1776, George Washington Greene. While Washington had slept in New Jersey more than any other state except his own Virginia, this was one residence where he definitely did not!

As Jane traversed the perimeter of this parlor, she experienced a continual shifting of apparitions, all of which vanished too suddenly to be definable. She seemed to hear the murmur of an unknown voice. It was strangely indistinct, however, and less articulate words than an unshaped sound, such as would be the utterance of feeling and sympathy, rather than of intellect.

Once more, our resident spirit, whomever it may have been, appeared to pause at the head of the staircase. Halting twice in its descent, it finally hesitated at the foot of the staircase. Each time, the delay seemed to be without reason, but was rather a forgetfulness of the purpose that had set it in motion. Alternately, it was as if the person's feet came involuntarily to a standstill because the motive power was too feeble to sustain its

Formal dances in the 18th century could be highly ritualized social activities, with prescribed rules of conduct and movements. George Washington was said to have greatly enjoyed such diversions and was capable of moving his large frame with surprising grace.
Gordon Bond

What creatures lurk in the mists of Dead Man's Pond near the Van Veighten House?

progress.

Finally, it made a long stop at the threshold of the parlor door. It took hold of the doorknob, and then loosened its grasp, without opening it. It felt as if a ghost was about to enter the room. The final pause at the threshold proved so long, that I, unable to endure the suspense any longer, rushed forward and threw open the door. No one was there. Even Jane agreed that it was time to leave.

It was late afternoon as we made our way from the Van Veighten House. Before returning to our car, we took a walk to the front of the house that faces Dead Man's Pond, a swampland fed by the Raritan River, containing an oxbow or elbow pond. A heavy mass of clouds obscured the sky, painting the entire scene with a grayish twilight tint. Despite this, we had no trouble seeing a huge shadow moving back and across the pond, seemingly watching us from a distance with its mysterious eyes. Neither one of us could figure out what it was.

As we observed in silence, the biggest, most frightening birdlike creature, with the blackest eyes imaginable, came gliding across the pond directly toward us. It looked like it had fur on its body, rather than feathers, and had a long swan-like neck, with a wingspan of about ten feet. It appeared to have long curved claws that reached out toward us, making this one fearful animal apparition!

I grabbed Jane's hand and together we ran for the car. The creature issued a noise that sounded like a bone-chilling mysterious wail. It followed us half way up Van Veighten Road, until its moaning sound finally disappeared into the distance. Thank goodness we could run faster than it could fly. Jane named the creature "Hessie" after the fearsome British mercenary Hessians, the king's detested hirelings. I told her she could keep her sense of humor. I just never wanted to see whatever it was again!

The Jacob Vanderveer House

Village of Pluckemin, Bedminster, New Jersey

King Charles II depicted by Sir Peter Lely, c. 1682.

The idyllic countryside of fertile rolling hills watered by the North Branch of the Raritan and Lamington Rivers that comprises Bedminster Township was settled shortly after Somerset County was formed in 1688. Title to the land was conveyed to East Jersey Proprietors Dr. John Johnstone and George Willocks of Perth Amboy, whose grant of some 11,000 acres here would be known as the "Peapack Patent" of 1701, the foundation of most of the land titles in Bedminster ever since. "Who were the Proprietors of East Jersey?" questioning Jane wanted to know.

In March 1664, Stuart King Charles II of England gave his brother James, the Duke of York (later King James II) all of Dutch-occupied New Jersey. With lavish generosity, the Duke of York in turn granted what is now New Jersey to John, Lord Berkeley and Sir George Carteret on June 23, 1664.

These two Proprietors had served the royal cause of Restoration in England during the trying years of the Civil War and the Commonwealth. The Duke bestowed the name *Nova Caesarea* or *New Jersey* in sentimental gratitude.

James, Duke of York (later King James II) as depicted by the studio of Studio of Sir Godfrey Kneller, c. 1680s.

John, Lord Berkeley

Sir George Carteret

Philip Carteret

Carteret had stoutly defended the Isle of Jersey in the English Channel for the Royalists during the English Civil War, in 1649, which had temporarily unseated the Stuarts from the English throne.

On February 10, 1665, Carteret and Berkeley chose Philip Carteret, a fourth cousin of Sir George, to be their New Jersey resident governor. Years later, on July 1, 1676, New Jersey was divided into East and West Jersey.

The Proprietors–Berkeley for West Jersey and Carteret for East Jersey–had extensive and exclusive powers. Except for certain restrictions in their individual charters, Proprietors were given authority almost as great as the king over their royal provinces. They could appoint public officials, create courts, issue laws, and impose customs, dues and regulations. Most importantly, they owned the land and could sell it, lease it, or collect quit-rents or fees from its occupants.

In order to pay the debts left by the death of Sir George Carteret on January 14, 1680, Lady Elizabeth sold the Province of East Jersey for £3,400 at the beginning of February 1682. The purchasers were William Penn and eleven English associates.

Very shortly thereafter, twelve other men, half of them from Scotland, were brought into the project. Thus, East Jersey became the common property of "Twenty Four Proprietors," twenty of whom were members of the Society of Friends (Quakers). The Duke of York issued a patent confirming their rights to both soil and government in March 1683.

Perth Amboy, founded November 23, 1683, became the capital of the province, the home of the resident Proprietors and headquarters of the East Jersey Board of Proprietors. Between 1683 and 1688 it was the port of entry for both Quaker and Calvinist Scottish non-conformists, serving their terms as indentured servants. Jointly sponsored by the Scottish Proprietors, many were from prisons, such as Bass Rock prison outside Edinburgh.

The last Scottish expedition of colonization, by promoter Sir George Scott, arrived in Perth Amboy in December 1685, on the ship *Henry and Francis*. Sir George and his wife Lady Margaret died during the voyage, but their daughter Euphemia Scott married fellow passenger and Proprietor Dr. John Johnstone. Johnstone rose to become one of the most prominent men in the colony prior his death in 1732. Jane was amazed to learn that the first Scottish colony in North America was right here in East Jersey.

The coat of arms of the Earl or Perth features a red wave pattern on a yellow field.

The grateful Scots who had immigrated to Ambo Point called their capital New Perth in honor of one of the Twelve Proprietors, James Drummond, the Earl of Perth, Scotland; older residents gave ground in the compromise name of Perth Amboy.

In 1688, the Roman Catholic King, James II, abdicated the throne during the English "Glorious" Revolution, and Lord Perth fled to France. Organized Scottish emigration ceased with Governor Robert Barclay's death in 1690. The Proprietors then turned to promoting the East Jersey settlement among the Dutch farming areas of Brooklyn and Manhattan. "The Lowlands above the Raritan are the handsomest, pleasantest country a man can behold," said Cornelius Van Tienhoven, Secretary of Nieuw Nederland in 1650. These thoughts were shared by many Dutch families who later migrated to that area.

Gerardus Beekman, from Belgium, whose family was among the first to settle Manhattan, then known as part of *Nova Belgique*, was one of the first to buy a vast tract of land in present day Franklin Township, Somerset County. This initiated a second phase of colonization in the upper Raritan Valley. Although the Scottish Proprietors' schemes for colonization lasted only a few short years, the initial settlement continued to attract new Scottish immigrants. This established the East Jersey Midlands as key places of Scottish influence within the Middle Colonies.

Questions raised in the seventeenth century about

**Queen Anne in a 1705
portrait by Michael Dahl.**

the legality of the Proprietors' right to govern were resolved on April 15, 1702 when Dr. John Johnstone, as a member of the East Jersey Board of Proprietors, signed a document ceding the Proprietors' powers back to the Crown and Queen Anne. However, the Proprietors retained their rights to the land, and continued to be prominent in New Jersey government, receiving important appointments from the Crown. The two Jerseys (West and East) were now united to form a single Royal Province under one Royal Governor. "So that is how New Jersey began," Jane said.

The Proprietors of East Jersey lost little time in exploiting their holdings. By 1702, they had voted themselves handsome dividends amounting to a total of 17,500 acres apiece. East Jersey thus acquired large landholders along the Raritan and Millstone Rivers, in Monmouth County and elsewhere, with estates commonly numbering a thousand or more acres.

After the War for Independence, the State of New Jersey adopted a policy of recognizing land titles from any longtime occupant of the land. To this day, the vast tracts of land still existing in Bedminster Township are a legacy of the large landowning Proprietors.

The Jacobus Vanderveer House is located on Routes 202/206. Route 206 is the main artery that connects Princeton, Somerville and Morristown. Seventeenth century roads in this area first followed Indian footpaths, which were later widened through use to accommodate wagons. In spite of the Scottish and English Proprietors' support for improvements after 1700, most New Jersey roads were made of dirt for over a century.

Situated on the 218 acres that make up River Road Park, Bedminster Township, this historic site is listed on the National and State Registers of Historic Places. It is a veritable Rosetta Stone of interpretation, as the headquarters for General Henry Knox, for history of the Pluckemin Encampment, Artillery Park and the

Vanderveer family—all-important components of New Jersey's pivotal role in the American Revolutionary War.

Sometime in 1743 Jacobus Vanderveer, the elder, whose grandfather had come to New York from North Holland in 1659, became the first Vanderveer to venture to settle in Bedminster. The Jacobus Vanderveer House is the last surviving building associated with the Vanderveer family in Bedminster.

Aside from their civic and religious contributions, the Vanderveer family members were staunch supporters of the American struggle for independence. Elias Vanderveer, "an active and spirited Whig," was taken prisoner during the British cavalry raid on Pluckemin in 1776. He was held captive under brutal conditions in one of the notorious prison ships anchored in New York harbor.

The most notorious of all the prison ships, the HMS *Jersey*, an old British man-of-war built in 1719, held more than 1,000 men at a time below decks. Even though the British had insisted that the *Jersey* had "a variety of apartments for officers and plenty of room between decks for men," in reality its captives were barely fed—on spoiled provisions. The prisoners quickly became "walking skeletons," dressed in rags and covered from head to toe with filth and lice. Racked by yellow fever, typhus and dysentery, many

The notorious British prison ship HMS *Jersey*, depicted in 1782 when it was being used to hold American prisoners of war under terrible conditions.

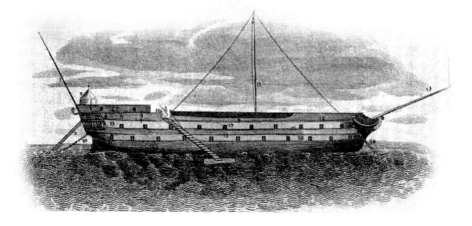

The Vanderveer House

died in their own bloody excrement and were buried a dozen at a time in shallow graves on the shores of Wallabout Bay.

Based in part on the bones that were collected twenty years after the war's end, most authorities agree that some 11,000 men perished aboard the prison ships. After Elias Vanderveer's release in 1778, he returned home, only to die in his thirty-third year on November 29, 1778.

A portion of the house of Dr. Henry Vanderveer, his brother, was later moved to East Jersey Olde Towne in Piscataway. Lawrence Vanderveer, whose house is in Hillsborough, served as a surgeon during the war and was also taken prisoner by the British. Jacobus Vanderveer, the younger, is known to have helped supply the American army.

The National and State registered Historic District of Pluckemin, situated in Bedminster Township, is located on lands that formerly belonged to Jacob Eoff, an early tavern keeper from Holland. He purchased some 500 acres of land from the estate of Dr. John Johnstone of Perth Amboy in 1741. The original Royal Charter creating Bedminster Township on April 4, 1749, is only one of two extant New Jersey township charters issued during the reign of King George II, and is owned by the Forbes family, who reside there.

A well traveled crossroads, the village of Pluckemin became an important center during the colonial and Revolutionary War periods. "It certainly is a charming village to this day," Jane said.

According to local tradition General Henry Knox and his wife Lucy lived in the Jacobus Vanderveer House from December 11, 1778 to June 3, 1779, while the general commanded the Continental Artillery encamped nearby at Artillery Park (now a suburban housing complex called The Hills).

To minimize the immediate impact of about 10,000 men of the Continental Army, equal to the entire population of Somerset County, brigades were assigned to locations several miles apart. The Artillery Camp of about 1,000 troops was located on the south side of the Second Watchung Mountain, secure from British attack, near the Jacobus Vanderveer House.

The Artillery Camp that General Knox established, the first military academy in the country for the training of artillery and engineer officers, was the forerunner of the Academy at West Point. Here Knox directed his troops in military strategy and tactics, and in the use of heavy artillery. "And to think that it is all covered over by a real estate development, what a loss," Jane sighed.

At six feet tall, Knox was a conspicuous sight. He weighted perhaps 250 pounds, was very gregarious, and had a booming voice. Boston born, he was the seventh of ten sons of Mary Campbell and William Knox, Scots-Irish Presbyterians.

A Boston bookseller by trade, Knox had a natural love of books and an interest in "the military art," as did his patrons John Adams and Nathanael Greene. It was at Knox's bookstore that he and Greene became

Knox and his men dragged fifty heavy cannon and assorted ammunition from Fort Ticonderoga, in New York, shown below, to Boston's Dorchester Heights in the dead of winter. Such exploits earned him the respect of George Washington.

Martha Washington led the celebrations at the Artillery Camp's pavilion in honor of the first anniversary of America's alliance with France's King Louis XVI (below).

friends. Like Greene, he was a man of marked ability, and Washington took note of this from the start of the war. Under the most trying conditions and through the darkest hours, Knox proved an outstanding leader, capable of accomplishing almost anything. Moreover, similar to Greene, he remained steadfastly loyal to Washington. "Loyalty is a quality hard to find and greatly to be admired," Jane said.

Knox served with distinction in nearly every major engagement of the war, from the Boston Massacre to the surrender at Yorktown, and later became George Washington's Secretary of War. During the siege of Boston, he and his men transported more than sixty tons of weaponry–shells and about fifty heavy guns–from Fort Ticonderoga to Dorchester Heights in the dead of winter. The heavy artillery took General Sir William Howe completely by surprise, helping persuade the British to abandon Boston on St. Patrick's Day, 1776 and sail north to Nova Scotia. Knox is also remembered as the first commander of West Point, and as the namesake for Fort Knox.

Profane, outspoken, and fond of good living, Knox often hid the fact that he had blown off two fingers in a hunting accident by constantly wrapping his mutilated hand in a handkerchief. He survived the dangers of the battlefield, only to die a strange death– at the age of fifty-six a chicken bone perforated his intestines.

The Artillery Camp was an impressive sight. In addition to well-built barracks for the enlisted men, and separate quarters for the officers, the camp included an armorer's shop, a complete military forge, and a laboratory. There was also an E-shaped building at its center.

On February 18, 1779 Knox hosted a ball at the Artillery Camp in a hundred-foot-long pavilion that was built for the occasion, the highlight of which included fireworks. The event honored the first anniversary of the alliance with King Louis XVI of

France and the American colonies. More than 300 people attended it, including Generals George Washington, Nathanael Greene, and a "circle of brilliants," led by Martha Washington.

The West Georgian wing of the Jacobus Vanderveer House, which is the oldest part built, between 1772 and 1778, is typical of the Dutch style frame houses that once dotted the Somerset County landscape before the Revolution. One wall in the southwest parlor features raised wood paneling above the fireplace, with a barrel-back cabinet to the side. The spacious east Federal addition, circa 1813, contains higher ceilings and a period New Jersey mantelpiece of the same era. It was during this time that the house reached its architectural apex. Jane and I marveled at how competently this house has been restored.

It was evident to us that the legacy of the Jacobus Vanderveer House provides an important link between Revolutionary War sites in Morristown and Somerville, chronicling the history of Washington's winter encampments and and the sacrifices he and his men made so that we can live in a free country. It continues to be, as it has for over two centuries, at the center of Bedminster Township's rich history.

The Abraham Staats House

ane was fifteen minutes early. We met on Barber Boulevard, facing the front façade of the Dutch Colonial mansion, which had been built in three sections in 1690, 1740 and 1825 in South Bound Brook, formerly a sleepy Dutch hamlet. Jane wore a broad smile as she exclaimed, "I promised I wouldn't be late!"–defying her perennial reputation.

It was a cool, sunny day. The lingering effects from a recent September hurricane had all passed away. I asked Jane if the low humidity could interfere with her ability to perceive psychic impressions. "To the contrary, she explained. It's a general misunderstanding. Actually heavy moisture, storms or the like work against receptivity, that's been my experience. A day like today is picture perfect to do an investigation," As I was anxious that the process would go well, I was excited to learn this. "How do we get into this place?" Jane now seriously inquired. I explained that we would need to go around the block to the entrance on Von Steuben Lane. Docents of the Friends Association were waiting to greet us, eagerly anticipating just what Jane's investigation would uncover. They would not be disappointed!

Before entering the mansion, I asked Jane if she were ready to begin. She then explained that she had psychically prepared herself to enter into the reality of the unseen. The process begins with meditation and deep relaxation, training the body to focus on the inner mind and to enter into a deeper state of consciousness. "It's a mystic gift which we all have," she said. And with a friendly smile she added, "It just needs to be developed!"

It was about two o'clock in the afternoon when we entered the revolutionary headquarters through a rear entrance. "Which way?" Jane asked.

"I want to go to the right!" she said. As we entered into the oldest part of the mansion in a nonchalant manner, the unsuspected things that Jane was to uncover made it all the more credible.

Reenactors portray a meeting with von Steuben at the Staats House.

The mansion was built in four distinct sections. We were now in the rear parlor of the original house, where General Friedrich, Baron von Steuben, had stayed when he used the Abraham Staats House as his headquarters during the time of the Second Middlebrook Encampment of the American Revolutionary War in 1778-79. We had gathered as a group of people eager to learn from the other side what we could of those events long shrouded in the darkness of the distant past. "Why do I see troops in formation out on the lawn?" Jane asked. At this point, I let out a conscious sigh.

We had told Jane nothing of the history of the mansion. It was here, I explained, that General Baron von Steuben trained and drilled George Washington's troops. They had then participated in a "Grand Review" in May 1779, at a reception and dinner for the visiting French Ambassador, Conrad Girard, the Spanish Envoy, Don Juan de Miralles, and other dignitaries, including Generals Washington and Knox.

When Jane spoke, it was as if telescopic eyes were looking at us from all directions, and as if Jane had wandered out of life into the distant past. This world is not a conclusion, I thought. Our species stands beyond, invisible as music, as positive as sound. "I feel the presence of several men here. They are charting, mapping, and writing as they consult about a war," she said. "There is a woman in colonial dress, full skirt and a bonnet—an older woman, a widow."

At this point Jane needed to know more about General von Steuben and his importance to the patriot cause. I went on to explain that he had been a Prussian officer who had served with distinction in the Seven Years' War, where he learned tactics and how to establish army discipline. His service had been commendable enough that he was eventually given a position as a General Staff Officer under Frederick II, King of Prussia, also known as Frederick the Great.

Invited by Congress, Baron von Steuben arrived at Portsmouth, New Hampshire, on December 1, 1777. He generously offered his assistance as a volunteer, stating that he wished no immediate compensation and would stake his fortunes upon the success of the American Revolutionary War. His assignment was to systematize the drill and tactics of the Continental Army. He was commissioned as a major general on April 26, 1778.

The importance of General Baron von Steuben's efforts at whipping the raw, undisciplined Americans into soldiers should not be underestimated. His "Blue Book" provided an ordered stucture serving as the basis for the emerging armed forces of the new United States.

The results of von Steuben's army training were in evidence during the Battle of Monmouth on June 28, 1778. Earlier, Washington had recommended the appointment of von Steuben as Inspector General of all the armies of the United States. Congress approved it on May 5, 1778. During the next winter von Steuben prepared "Regulations for the Order and Discipline of the Troops of the United States," also known as the "Blue Book," which was of great value to the army.

Baron von Steuben continued to lend assistance during the revolution at Valley Forge, the Battle of Monmouth, and later during the command in Virginia and the Southern Campaign. Due to an illness in April 1781, the Marquis de Lafayette superseded him in command of Virginia. However, he rejoined the army for the final campaign at Yorktown, where he was commander of one of the three divisions of Washington's troops to whom British Lord Cornwallis surrendered. He was discharged from the military with honors on March 24, 1784.

"History has many treasures and certainly the Abraham Staats House is one of these," Jane said, her psychic impressions having now come across larger than life. "You are getting results that far exceeded our expectations. It is incredibly satisfying," I said. "Yes, what a totally unique experience to be in the very space occupied by one of the most influential leaders of the American Revolution," Jane replied.

Feeling a sense of psychic urgency, and without looking backward, Jane then turned and led the way to the front entrance door, standing with us in the stillness of the hall, admiring its age. The door is split horizontally across the middle to allow the top portion to open, thus permitting light and air in, and keeping livestock out. The door still contains the hand-blown bull's eye glass windows noted by many colonial visitors to the house. Over the course of many years, that door has been opened and closed thousands of time by hands that no longer have living witnesses. It was quiet, and during the silence we moved slowly into the handsome front parlor, entranced by the accuracy of Jane's narrative and eager to be transported further into her world of the invisible. Here Jane told us that she felt the presence of an important lady, a hostess who was attended by servants, and who was receiving foreign guests. "they're having a lively conversation," Jane said.

Slowly, as if in a trance, Jane walked around the perimeter of the room, moving idly until she reached the large paneled corner fireplace. "I have a sense of important papers being signed in this room—some kind of agreement or orders." Our group understood, knowing that von Steuben and Washington had met here with the French Ambassador and Spanish Envoy in May 1779. As Jane now moved along the east wall to a built-in corner cupboard she told us, "There is a lady here serving tea to important guests." Martha Washington had accompanied her husband here many times and was always a gracious hostess. How hospitable, I thought, of Martha to be serving tea!

The front door of the Staats House features unique hand-blown bull's eye glass windows.

The Abraham Staats House

Martha Custis had been a widow at the time she married Washington in January, 1759. She brought to the marriage a sizable fortune which, combined with Washington's inheritance, made him one of the richest men in colonial America.

Stepping into the original colonial kitchen, Jane felt the presence of servants of African descent. "I see clothes being dried on a line here and a woman named Bessie or Betty." In the loft above, Jane sensed the presence of a husband and wife. "The woman is tending a baby, the owners' baby," Jane concluded. The couple's spirits were so close by; it was as if she could almost touch them. I thought, "They're here."

"Why am I getting the name Abraham?" Jane wanted to know. "He's an angry man," she added. "It was Abraham Staats who lived here with his family during the American Revolutionary War," I explained. Staats was a prominent landowner and citizen of his community, laboring as a farmer while teaching mathematics, surveying and navigation. He was also an ardent patriot. After the war, Abraham served as a tax collector for Somerset County. "That explains it," Jane replied with a giggle, "not a happy job!"

"Who's Henry?" Jane asked. It was Henry (or in Dutch, Hendrick) Staats who is believed to have built the central portion of the colonial farmhouse, circa 1740, using what is called "Dutch" architecture. How incredible it was to think that Jane was in touch with this long-absent owner, but she was.

Unaccountably strange, centuries after the fact, Jane told us that she saw horses tied up outside this kitchen waiting to be ridden. "There is an African man who rides from here on a mission and then returns with information. Does that make any sense?" Jane wanted to know. "Yes!" I said. "A slave in the Staats household known as 'Tory Jack' reputedly helped the patriot cause by spying on the British Crown forces in the area and then reporting back to the Americans. He would ride and return from here to New Brunswick to spy where British troops were garrisoned in inns and homes."

Tory Jack's rides would take him past the 1688 home of Hendrick Fisher. As President of the New Jersey Provincial Congress, Hendrick Fisher read the Declaration of Independence to a gathering of local people on July 9, 1776, at the Frelinghuysen Tavern in Raritan, New Jersey. Known as the Samuel Adams of New Jersey, the British had standing orders to hang him on sight.

As we were busy enjoying the unique history of the place, the hours had quickly passed by. Yet there was more to see and experience. We proceeded to the large east wing, built by Staats' son Isaac in 1825, using money he had gained from the sale of land to create that portion of the Delaware and Raritan Canal that flows past the property.

As if spirits were hovering around the dining room, now flooded in bright sunlight, Jane announced, "I'm getting several impressions here. I see women in long dresses. They're waltzing and having a ball. It's a large group," Jane added. It now felt as if we were standing between two worlds, only these phantom dancers were bodiless! We heard no low murmuring of voices, nor felt any lonesome drafts. These invisible dancers were for us eternally lost from view.

Writing the Declaration of Independence was only the beginning. In order for it to be disseminated to the people, it needed to be printed. This is one of the first printings by John Dunlap–known as a "Dunlop Broadside"–from the Yale University Beinecke Rare Book and Manuscript Library. Hendrick Fisher would have read a printed copy like this to his neighbors in New Jersey.

Jane continued, "Was this room used for meetings? I see a gavel on a table and some kind of business meeting taking place." A member of the Friends Association explained that in the nineteenth century there were no public buildings in this area. Groups would meet in houses with large rooms like this.

As we passed through the 1939 add-on doorway into the present kitchen, Jane saw children–two girls and a boy–playing. "There was a very loving family who lived here," she said. "I see them having holiday dinners." "Fortunately, the residents of the Abraham Staats House have always cared for this residence and we are fortunate to have it in this condition," our guide said.

Before ending our tour, Jane asked to investigate the cellar. I stood before the cellar door, not daring to open it in case a face I had never seen might be lurking there! Jane opened it, and we cautiously followed behind her. A chilly peace infected the catacomb-like basement. Nobody was there. "It's not here," Jane insisted. "What's not here?" I replied, relieved it was not a "who"! "The buried treasure," Jane insisted. "Somewhere under this house are valuable coins in a metal container. Could they be some undeclared tax monies collected by Abraham Staats?"

Rockingham

The history of Rockingham began when Jedidiah Higgins had a small two-story farmhouse, with one room on each floor, built between 1702 and 1710. The house was expanded in 1760 by Judge John Berrien, a prosperous farmer appointed Judge of Somerset County in 1739 and Justice of the New Jersey Provincial Supreme Court in 1764. Berrien's grandfather was Jansen Berrien, a native of Berrien in the French Department of Finisterre. Jansen Berrien was a Huguenot fugitive who fled France for Holland, and finally ended up in Flatbush, Long Island in 1669.

Rockingham

In the spring of 1783, the Continental Congress, struggling with the burden of war debts, was driven from Philadelphia by the threat of mutinous soldiers furious about not receiving their back pay, rations or sufficient clothing. On June 26, 1783, the Continental Congress made Princeton the *de facto* capital of the new nation, until it adjourned in early November.

As peace negotiations dragged on into 1783, the army, quartered at Newburgh on the Hudson River, had grown restive. Congress summoned Washington from his Newburgh, New York headquarters on August 12 to discuss the dissolution of the army.

There was no available residence in Princeton in mid-August to accommodate Washington, his wife Martha, and his staff. As a result, Rockingham, in nearby Rocky Hill, was chosen as his last wartime headquarters, from August 23 to November 10, 1783. Furnished in period

Elias Boudinot served as President of the Continental Congress from 1782 to 1783 and as the Director of the United States Mint from 1795 until 1805.

pieces and replica military objects, Rockingham interprets a family residence shifted into personal use by the Commander-in-Chief. Beautifully restored, Jane felt right at home in Washington's final headquarters.

Margaret Berrien, the widow of Judge Berrien, knew, as did the Continental Congress, that Washington's campaigns in Central New Jersey had been crucial to the development of his national reputation. She was pleased beyond measure to have such distinguished company, as well as a lease paid for by the Congress (although there is no record of her ever having been paid).

During this time, Congress met in the Library Room of Nassau Hall in Princeton. Sessions were presided over by Elias Boudinot, one of New Jersey's most distinguished political leaders. Boudinot later served in the Federal Congress and as the Director of the United States Mint. (In 1816 he was also a founder of the American Bible Society.) The highlight of this 1783 session was the ten-week visit of General Washington, who consulted with Congress on the final arrangements for the demobilization of the army.

It was at Rockingham that Washington, feeling relaxed and even witty, entertained members of Congress at dinner. The Washingtons were visited by Elias Boudinot, and in turn made frequent visits at Morven in Princeton, where Boudinot was staying with his sister, Annis Stockton, the widow of Richard Stockton.

Other Rockingham visitors included Thomas Paine, who, it was supposed, had written a letter saying the country wasn't as mindful of his services as it should be; John Paul Jones, the Scottish expatriate and one of the greatest fighters in the United States Navy; Thomas Jefferson, who may have demonstrated that the cunning and cruelty of politics could sometimes be balanced by such simplicities as playing the violin; and Congressman James Madison.

It was also here that George Washington sat for

portrait painter William Dunlap of Perth Amboy, who is often considered by theatre historians as the father of American drama. During this portrait sitting, the pleasant circumstances of Rockingham must have been in marked contrast to all that was in Washington's mind. Jane could sense Washington as he recollected the years of his service here.

On June 16, 1775 the Second Continental Congress had unanimously elected Washington as the Commander-in-Chief of the Continental Army and of the forces "raised or to be raised, for the defense of American liberty." John Adams, who had nominated Washington for the post of supreme commander, remembered Washington accepting the nomination at the State House in Philadelphia.

John Adams had suggested to the Continental Congress that Washington was "a gentleman whose skill as an officer, whose independent fortune, great talents and universal character would command the respect of America and unite the full exertions of the Colonies better than any other person alive..." His cousin Samuel Adams seconded the motion. "It's obvious to me that John Adams really admired George Washington," Jane said.

Adams had never been a soldier, but Washington had already seen duty. Washington would recall his military service as William Dunlap carefully brushed the pigment onto the canvas of his famous masterpiece. He would recollect November 6, 1752, when he was appointed by the governor of Virginia as a major in the Virginia militia, at the age of twenty, and was sent to the wilds of western Pennsylvania. There he had served with the militia during the French and Indian War at the Battle of Fort Necessity on July 3, 1754, and challenged the French claim to the Allegheny River Valley. He survived four bullets through his coat and two horses shot out from under

As William Dunlap created this portrait of George Washington around 1783, the sitter was at a crossroads in his public life, between soldier and political leader of a new nation.

George Washington as painted by Charles Willson Peale in 1779.

him. By August 14, 1755, he had been appointed Colonel and Commander of the Virginia Regiment.

Virginia was one of the most radical of the colonies, and Fairfax County, where Washington lived, was one of the state's most radical counties. On August 1, 1774, Washington was elected to the First Continental Congress, and that autumn Fairfax County organized a militia of its own, with Washington elected as its commander.

At the Second Continental Congress, in 1775, Washington headed four committees on military matters and supplies. He had cut an impressive figure, a combination of *noblesse oblige* and modesty, and he had offered to serve without pay, asking only that Congress cover his expenses. His sixteen years in the House of Burgesses, plus his experience in the Continental Congress, had educated him in the political process. He respected the authority of the Congress.

Therefore, it was with the utmost seriousness that Washington, at age forty-three, while accepting the nomination as Commander-in-Chief, remarked, "I am truly sensible of the high Honor done me. I will enter upon the momentous duty, and exert every power I possess for the support of the glorious cause... But I beg it may be remembered by every gentleman in the room, that I this day declare with the utmost sincerity, I do not think myself equal to the Command I am honored with." (Even those who had their doubts knew Washington had meant every word of it).

With his only prior experience in backwoods

warfare, he had never led an army into battle, never commanded anything larger than a regiment, and never directed a siege. In March 1776, Washington would lead the Continental Army to victory in Boston, when his army took Dorchester Heights. And on April 3, 1776 Harvard College, in a show of appreciation, would award him the first of five honorary degrees. Jane felt the sense of relief that the British no longer threatened the New Englanders.

Washington reviewing his troops at Valley Forge.

During his sitting for another portrait, this time painted by Charles Willson Peale, Washington allowed his mind to drift toward the Millstone River. Here he had led his troops after the Battles of Trenton and Princeton, along the river roads and back to Morristown to spend the winter of 1777. Smallpox had dropped hundreds of the valiant in the January snows there. He also thought back to the bitter winter of 1779-1780, when he occupied the mansion formerly owned by Jacob Ford, Jr. (the first National Historic Park in the country). He could recall how New Jersey had sheltered his army through four years and three winters and how its land had been ravaged as no other state had been.

From Morristown's strategic location, the large British force in New York City could be observed from a place where the American army could be safeguarded through the difficult winter months. When the army had arrived at their quarters in Jockey Hollow the snow was already two feet deep. Crossing the Hudson on the thick ice from Manhattan to Paulus Hook was "practicable for the heaviest Cannon, an Event unknown in the Memory of Man," British General Pattison wrote to Lord George Germain.

During that winter of 1780, more than twenty successive snowstorms had covered the hills and slopes with six- or seven-foot snowdrifts. The cold

"Give 'em Watts, boys!"
The Rev. James Caldwell's wife, Hannah, had been shot at the Battle of Connecticut Farms (now Union Township). The British said it was a stray American shot. The Americans said she had been killed in cold blood by a Hessian, shot through an open window as she held her child on a bed, with her maid and other child beside her. The murder of a clergyman's wife was fodder for American propaganda for months. Only sixteen days later, Rev. Caldwell (who had been with Washington at Morristown) was at the Battle of Springfield, handing out copies of Watt's hymnals from the Presbyterian Churc h – not for reading, but so they could use the paper from the torn out pages as wadding for their muskets!

was so intense and so prolonged that streams froze, and local mills could not grind grain for the starving troops. Ill-clad soldiers, lacking the barest of protection from the cold, and with frozen hands and feet, experienced more cruel privations by far than did those who served at Valley Forge.

Washington could call to mind the sudden raid by some 7,375 men under General Wilhelm von Knyphausen from Staten Island on June 7, 1780, which culminated in the Battle of Connecticut Farms, and the subsequent Second Battle of Springfield on June 23, 1780. Here General Greene had led 2,500 Continental troops, later aided by 5,000 New Jersey militia rallied by General Philemen Dickinson, to oppose Knyphausen's 6,000 British and Hessian soldiers.

The Reverend James Caldwell, whose wife Hannah had been murdered sixteen days earlier, had passed out Watts' hymnals for use as wadding in American cannons. His shout "Give them Watts, boys!" still echoed through the years. The Revolutionary War in the north, which had been waged furiously for four years, came to an end in New Jersey with the Second Battle of Springfield.

Washington thought of the success of Sir Henry Clinton in the Southern Campaign at Savannah, Charleston, King's Mountain, Cowpens, and elsewhere, which had been quelled by increasingly bad news. Clinton had left Cornwallis in charge of the Southern Campaign and retired to New York City, where he expected Washington would stage a major battle. Washington, in fact, had prepared misleading dispatches that he hoped would fall into Clinton's hands. The ploy worked, and Clinton had been completely fooled.

Washington then contemplated one of his boldest gambles of all, which took place in August of 1781. Leaving behind only a few regiments to monitor the British garrison in New York City, he and his French ally, Jean Baptiste Donatien de Vimeur, the Comte de

Rochambeau, led a combined force of 7,000 American and French soldiers which converged at the town of Princeton. They then marched southward to Yorktown, Virginia, to trap the British army of Lord Cornwallis on the Yorktown Peninsula.

Cornwallis relied on the Royal Navy to rescue him via the Chesapeake Bay, but the French had blocked its entrance with twenty-eight ships that had arrived just in time from the French West Indies. With the aid of the French fleet under Admiral de Grasse, the Americans had a chance for a surprise attack and victory at Yorktown. In London, the British Prime Minister, Lord North, would exclaim upon hearing the news, "Oh God! It's all over."

Cornwallis surrendered his army of some 7,000 soldiers and 900 seamen on October 19, 1781, while the Redcoats marched out onto the field near Yorktown in a ceremony of capitulation. Suitable to the occasion, their bands played "The World Turned Upside Down." Given the slow communications of the period, the news did not reach London until November 25, 1781.

The world did indeed turn upside down for the British at Yorktown, when one of the mightiest armies in the world surrendered to the ragtag provincials who made up the ranks of the American army.

As if to compound the irony of Britain's vast resources but terrible timing, as Yorktown fell on October 19, a fleet from London arrived in New York carrying a staggering amount of food: enough provisions to feed 30,000 men for six months.

The war continued for several more months, but by March 1782, with the resignation of Lord North, a new ministry in England was ready to yield to American demands. The provisional draft of a peace treaty was signed at Paris on November 30, 1782. However, it was not until September 3, 1783 that the final documents were signed, freeing the thirteen colonies from the bonds of Great Britain. "It was finally over," Jane exclaimed.

Washington remembered the cease-fire he had issued on April 9, 1783, thus ending the hostilities. Congress proclaimed war's end on April 15, 1783, six years plus two days after the surprise assault on the vastly outnumbered Americans at the Battle of Bound Brook. New Jersey church bells rang, summoning congregations together in thanksgiving.

Soldiers marching across the Jersey Midlands from 1776 to 1781 had wasted fields, torched homes, churches and barns, and generally terrorized the citizenry. Weed-covered ruins of buildings from the British occupation of 1776 were in evidence everywhere.

As wealthy Loyalists liquidated their assets–their homes in town and country, along with furniture and other contents–Perth Amboy became a magnet for patriot thieves, as nine-tenths of the city was burnt to the ground and destroyed. Many who had lost their land, possessions, and livelihoods to the rebels petitioned the British government to resettle them in England, Nova Scotia, on the St. John River in New Brunswick, Canada, or in the West Indies.

But New Jersey colonists could at last be proud of their monumental accomplishment. Throughout the colony, the common man had played his part in assuring this glorious victory. New Jersey patriots had contributed fully to the war effort by maintaining morale, organizing local militias, and thwarting British movements. They had fully demonstrated those qualities that were fundamental to securing the rights and privileges we now so highly cherish.

With the official conclusion of hostilities, conflicts arising from both its diversity and vastness were to be future sources of difficulty and strength for the new United States of America. The infant nation was already a physical empire. Its boundaries encompassed 889,000 square miles–in comparison, Spain, Great Britain and France totaled only a little over 500,000 square miles. Washington knew that size alone did not equal nationhood; only settlement and national cohesion could unite its inhabitants.

The news of the signing of the Treaty of Paris, and thus the winning of the War of Independence, reached Congress and Washington on October 31, 1783. The entire nation rejoiced that the United States of America had taken its rightful place among the nations of the world. The last British troops finally sailed from American harbors on November 25, 1783. This victory marked the end of the last effort of an English king to rule as well as reign.

The final version of Washington's "Farewell Orders to the Army of the United States" was written by one of Washington's aides-de-camp, David Cobb, who worked from notes, dictation and suggestions from Washington. In his "Farewell Orders" Washington bid his army "an affectionate, a long farewell." He recalled how a disciplined army had been formed, and how men from every one of the colonies had ultimately become "but one patriotic band of Brothers."

The "Farewell Orders" were dispatched from Rockingham to General Henry Knox at Newburgh, New York, with instructions that they were to be read to the troops there on November 2. Dr. Benjamin Rush, Signer of the Declaration of Independence,

David Cobb crafted Washington's "Farewell Orders" from the General's notes. He would go on to represent Massachusetts in the Congress.

observed "The American war is over, but that is far from the case with the American Revolution. On the contrary, nothing but the first act of that great drama is closed."

Five years later, on November 1, 1788, a disbanding Confederation Congress was to set in motion the mechanism by which future presidents would be elected. Early the next year, on April 6, 1789, George Washington was the unanimous choice of all sixty-nine electors and therefore the president-elect, with John Adams chosen as Vice President.

It was Washington alone who could pull together both the diversity and the vastness of the new nation. As a founder and Father of Our Country, he had somehow kept the military obedient to him and to Congress. He had helped bring about a transformation of the American government from the Articles of Confederation to the United States Constitution. His leadership and character still have the power to inspire, and his life is still worth emulating today.

Part Five

His Excellency, George Washington

The Cross Keys Tavern

Woodbridge, New Jersey

George Washington's last significant visit to New Jersey took place during his trip to New York City for his Presidential Inauguration. On April 16, 1789, he and his entourage left his home at Mount Vernon, Virginia, and headed north. It took them a full week to cover the 250-mile journey to New York City, the nation's original capital.

The party's plan was to be on the road by 5:30 a.m. each day, with travel taking place throughout the day. But at every major stop along the route— Baltimore, Wilmington, Philadelphia, Trenton, Princeton and New Brunswick—there were welcoming delegations and honor guards that flanked Washington's coach, official receptions and banquets, and speeches and toasts that required a response. Cannons boomed, bells rang, and bridges were draped with magnificent wreaths.

George Washington's New Jersey campaigns had been crucial to the development of his national reputation. The state, in effect, had become a second home for Washington, as he had fought more battles on its soil than anywhere else during the eight long years of the war. He had spent more time in New Jersey than in any other state, and it would retain a special place in his memory. The General would never forget the "Jerseys," nor would the Jersey people ever forget him.

Many historians call the Battle of Trenton the most important battle in American history. While addressing the New Jersey General Assembly at Trenton on December 6, 1783, Washington spoke of the people of the state who, after being overrun by the enemy, had rallied and driven the invader from their home.

William Patterson shown in the robes of a Supreme Court Justice, an office to which he was appointed by George Washington following Patterson's service as New Jersey's second governor.

In future years, Washington would certainly remember the warm reception he had been given at the Indian Queen Tavern in New Brunswick after he had said a final goodbye to his officers at Fraunces Tavern in New York City on December 4, 1783, before proceeding on to Trenton and later Mount Vernon.

Traveling once more across the Jersey Midlands, he may have been recalling the major role William Patterson (later the first of New Jersey's two Senators, second Governor of New Jersey and Associate Justice of the United States Supreme Court) and New Jersey had played in the development of the new United States Constitution on June 15, 1787. Patterson had been instrumental in New Jersey's leading the way to the United States bicameral system of government we enjoy today.

And so it was that "an admiring concourse" greeted Washington, the President-elect, as he entered Trenton on April 21, 1789. This crowd was memorialized in a Nathanael Currier lithograph depicting the general and his party passing under a flower-festooned archway, visibly touched by the message on the arch: THE DEFENDER OF THE MOTHERS WILL BE THE PROTECTOR OF THE DAUGHTERS. As Washington emerged from under the arch, little white-robed girls and their mothers, along with thirteen young women (each representing a different state) strewed flowers in Washington's path while singing an ode written especially for the occasion by Major Richard Howell. Howell later became the third governor of New Jersey (1793-1801).

St. James Episcopal Church, in a part of Piscataway that is now in Edison Township, hosted Washington for morning prayers on his way to New York.

Departing New Brunswick on Sunday, April 22, he proceeded on the King's Highway (Woodbridge Avenue, Route 514 East) to St. James Episcopal Church, Piscataway (now in Edison Township) for Morning Prayer. From its three—tiered pulpit both Samuel Seabury, the first Episcopal Bishop in America, and John Croes had preached. The Rt. Reverend John Croes, D.D. went on to be elected the first Episcopal

Bishop of New Jersey on August 15, 1815, at the Annual Convention at St. Michael's Church, Trenton. Bishop Croes had earlier served as a sergeant major during the American Revolution. Called to be Rector of Christ Church, New Brunswick, he remained there until his death in 1832.

After worshiping at St. James Church, Washington's entourage continued on what is now Route 514, journeying east through Bonhamtown, and crossing Poplar Hill and Fords (on present day Upper Main Street). Continuing on, they then crossed over Heard's Brook, as it babbled and gurgled below them, and entered the town of Woodbridge. The cheers of the local citizenry enveloped the Washington party, as the people sang the tune "Yankee Doodle" to them. The party stayed at the Cross Keys Tavern that evening.

The greeting George Washington received as he entered Trenton on his way to New York to take the oath of office as the United States' first President inspired Nathaniel Currier to create this lithograph.

The Cross Keys Tavern has become a lost historical treasure, as have so many other fine buildings of our historical and cultural past which have been neglected, forgotten, or destroyed. Moved one block north to Upper James Street, in the early 1920s, it still stands, its former prominent location now replaced with a Knights of Columbus clubhouse. "Yes, the Cross Keys Tavern stands virtually unnoticed today," Jane said.

The Cross Keys refer to the key roads leading to somewhere important. In this case, the key roads were the King's Highway, which led north to Elizabeth and Newark, or west to New Brunswick, Princeton, and Trenton; Amboy Avenue, which led south to the capital, Perth Amboy; and one last road, presently named Woodbridge Avenue, which led east to the coast and the Arthur Kill.

Woodbridge, New Jersey, was the scene of major fighting between British Tories and American Continentals during the Revolutionary War. It is the oldest original township in the state. It is named in honor of the Reverend John Woodbridge who, with a number of associates and their families, arrived there in the summer of 1665 from Newbury, Massachusetts. English Royal Governor Philip Carteret granted a charter to the 30,000-acre Township of Woodbridge on June 1, 1669.

On April 22, 1789, the first New Jersey State Governor, William Livingston of Liberty Hall (built in 1772) in Elizabethtown, New Jersey met with Washington at the Cross Keys Tavern. The Woodbridge Cavalry, commanded by Captain Ichabod Potter, escorted the celebrated visitor to the tavern, which at the time was kept by John Manning. Here Washington was given a tumultuous reception by a large military and civilian contingent.

Lined up to greet Washington were many of the surviving Woodbridge residents who had taken part in the struggle for independence during the twenty-nine skirmishes that occurred in the Woodbridge area. Among the notables were Brigadier General Nathaniel Heard (then Colonel Heard) who commanded the Middlesex County Militia, and who had arrested Royal Governor William Franklin on June 19, 1776, at the Proprietary House in Perth Amboy.

Washington surely reminisced about how in mid-January, 1776, the Continental Congress had sent Colonel Heard with 1,200 militia to suppress the Tories of Queens County, New York. Using a voter list, Heard's militia scoured Queens County for two weeks and administered a test oath to 800 Loyalists. In addition, he confiscated 1,000 muskets and arrested nineteen of the twenty-six most active Tory leaders.

Certainly on hand on that day in April was Major Zebulon Pike, a descendant of John Pike, who was among the original settlers of Woodbridge, as well as patriot Janet Pike Gage, who raised the first Liberty Pole to fly the Stars and Stripes for the first time at the Cross Keys Tavern in Woodbridge. (Her nephew, former Woodbridge resident General Zebulon Montgomery Pike, of War of 1812 fame, discovered 14,110-foot-high Pike's Peak in the Rocky Mountains, near Colorado Springs, Colorado, in 1806.)

The cemetery behind the Presbyterian "Old White Church" at Woodbridge is home to numerous historic graves.

Visiting Janet Gage's gravestone in the east side yard of the Woodbridge United Methodist Church, Jane felt a vast sense of emptiness. "There is no body buried here," she said. I then explained that Janet Gage's grave was covered over with asphalt in the early 1960s, and is now in a parking lot behind the Fellowship Hall of the Church. "What a crime," she said.

Many others from Woodbridge, who had served as officers in the Continental Army, were in attendance. They included Colonel Samuel Crow, General Clarkson Edgar, Captain David Edgar, Colonel Benjamin Brown, and Lieutenant James Paten, all of whose graves may now be found in the burying grounds of the First Presbyterian Church (Old White Church). Remembered was Captain Nathaniel Randolph (who had died of this wounds suffered at a skirmish near Springfield in 1780).

Also present was Woodbridge resident Dr. Moses Bloomfield, a well-to-do physician and political figure who had served in both the colonial New Jersey Provincial Assembly and the New Jersey Provincial Congress that replaced it at the beginning of the American Revolution. Descended from Thomas Bloomfield, a first settler of Woodbridge in 1665, he had served as surgeon in the Continental Army. Thomas Bloomfield, his ancestor, had been a

Boxwood Hall, where
Elias Boudinot
entertained Washington,
stands in Elizabeth.

major in Oliver Cromwell's army. When Charles II was restored as king, Bloomfield found himself on the losing side and fled to America.

Dr. Moses Bloomfield's son Joseph, also born in Woodbridge, was a major in the Continental Army, a lawyer, Attorney General and the fourth Governor of New Jersey (during the years 1801-02 and 1803-12). The town of Bloomfield, New Jersey, is named in his honor.

The Reverend Dr. Azel Roe, Pastor of the Old White Church (First Presbyterian Church) was also in attendance. He had preached independence from his pulpit, as had John Witherspoon of Princeton. A Scottish-born Presbyterian, Dr. Roe had no love for the English. He had taken part in one of the skirmishes at Blazing Star (now Carteret), and was captured by the British and imprisoned for a time at the Old Sugar House in New York City.

Washington left Woodbridge on April 23, and traveled to Rahway, where military companies from Newark, Connecticut Farms and Elizabethtown escorted him to Elizabethtown. Situated four miles from Newark, it was the first English and second permanent settlement in the state. In 1665, Philip Carteret, first Governor of East Jersey, landed at the point of land, which he named Elizabethtown, in honor of Lady Elizabeth Carteret, wife of Sir George Carteret. Because of its proximity to Staten Island, the town suffered greatly from Tory raids during the Revolution, and it was the scene of five battles or engagements in December 1776, January 25-30, 1777, July 21, 1778, June 6, 1780, and June 8, 1780.

Here, at Boxwood Hall, his home since 1772, Elias Boudinot, who served as the President of the Continental Congress from 1782 to 1783, entertained Washington and a committee from Congress. Afterwards Washington proceeded from Elizabeth Point on a crimson-canopied, forty-seven-foot barge propelled by uniformed oarsmen. It was followed by a flotilla of colorfully bedecked small craft across Newark and New York Bay, landing to a stupendous ovation at lower Manhattan. "All ranks and professions," ran one newspaper account, "expressed their feelings in loud acclamations, and with rapture hailed the arrival of the Father of His Country."

Conclusion

16

When George Washington, at age fifty-seven, was inaugurated in New York City on April 30, 1789, Robert R. Livingston, Chancellor of New York State and a former warden of Trinity Church, Wall Street, administered the oath of office. Trinity Church, as the Church of England, had been a bastion of royal power, and was, as now, the richest parish in the country. After the ceremony at Federal Hall, momentarily delayed by the absence of a Bible, the assembled crowd marched up Broadway to St. Paul's Chapel, which had been built in 1766. The chapel, located on Division Street (now Fulton), is today the oldest public building in continuous use in Manhattan, and is part of Trinity Parish.

Washington filed into the special pew prepared for him (a rebuilt facsimile is still set apart as Washington's Pew) and heard appropriate prayers for his success from the mouth of the first Episcopal Bishop of New York (and former rector of Trinity), Samuel Provoost, recently appointed chaplain of the country's Senate.

Later, in October 1789, the Episcopalians, meeting in their first General Convention in Philadelphia, adopted a resolution praising Washington as one "who has happily united a tender regard for other churches with an inviolable attachment to his own."

While two-thirds of the signers of the Declaration of Independence were Anglican, as a group they were by far the least patriotic segment of the colonial population. The church's connection to the British establishment had all but demolished it when the colonies fought that very establishment. An incredible 70,000 Anglicans fled the colonies during the war or immediately thereafter. The more prominent a citizen–merchant, landowner, or royal official–the more likely he was to leave the uncertain new nation.

George Washington, as the leader of a new national government, was also the leading representative of the power and prestige found in the property, ancestry and money of those self-same Anglican Loyalists who had fled to Canada or England. Soon after the Revolution, Anglicanism all but disappeared as a major religion, although it still held the allegiance of a small minority–the oldest, proudest and richest families in the country.

The newly formed Protestant Episcopal Church in the United States of America, whose form of service appealed strongly to Washington's sense of dignity, harmony, color and good taste, was to become the soul of the American upper class in the High Victorian age and well into the twentieth century.

Could Washington, who envisioned a "great church for national purposes in the capital city," ever have imagined the great Episcopal Cathedral of St. Peter and St. Paul towering above the City of Washington, D.C. from its stately site on Mount St. Alban? The cathedral had been incorporated into the 1791 plans for the Federal City prepared by Pierre Charles L'Enfant, the young French engineer and architect who had served as a volunteer in the Revolution. In 1893, the United States Congress granted a charter for the foundation that would build the sixth largest Gothic cathedral in the world. Our own version of Westminster Abbey, the National Cathedral is a semi-official repository of national pride, hope and national unity. Could Washington have imagined that in 1976, the completed nave would be dedicated at services that would bring Queen Elizabeth II of England, President Gerald Ford, the Archbishop of Canterbury, F.D. Coggan, and thousands of others to Mount St. Alban? Such was the rapprochement that was to occur between the United States and Great Britain.

One of the Memorial Bays on the main level of the Cathedral is Washington Bay, with its heroic statue of George Washington. The many facets of Washington's long career are reflected in the words carved on each side of the base: First Citizen, Churchman, President, Statesman, Farmer, Soldier, Patriot, and Freemason. The surrounding alcove is filled with carvings symbolic of Washington's life and achievements. The abstract stained glass window celebrates the founding of a new nation. Each color evokes an aspect of the search for freedom: the dark colors below represent tyranny; the reds signify the blood lost in the struggle; the greens symbolize the growing nation; and the blues bring to mind the open sky above the vast land. Finally, in the floor of the bay, is a seal representing each of the thirteen colonies.

Faced with sustained suffering, disease, hunger, desertion, cowardice, disillusionment, defeat and fear, the Revolution almost certainly would have failed without the leadership and unrelenting perseverance and character of George Washington. In the last analysis, it was the service of his Continental Army, largely in Central New Jersey, that had been the key to victory.

In retrospect, it would seem that the moment for which all the people of New Jersey had been preparing themselves for many decades had arrived. Arising from the humblest origins, a remarkably free and capable society, democratic in its social, economic, and political institutions, had taken form. Its vital and immeasurable contributions to the building of a new state and nation were much greater than its size and resources.

New Jersey had been home to Washington, the pride of his country and the terror of Great Britain. Here in New Jersey we can still go to those places where his soldiers fought, drowned, died and prevailed. We can step into their footsteps and appreciate them with understanding and sympathy. Moreover, we can glimpse them and all that their great sacrifice for the welfare of our national life represents.

Bibliography

Books

Beck, Henry Charlton. *The Jersey Midlands*. New Brunswick, N.J.: Rutgers University Press, 1962.

Bill, Alfred Hoyt. *New Jersey and the Revolutionary War*. New Brunswick, N.J.: Rutgers University Press, 1964.

Bowen, Catherine Drinker. *John Adams and the American Revolution*. Boston: Little, Brown and Company, 1950.

Brookhiser, Richard. *Founding Father: Rediscovering George Washington*. New York: Simon and Schuster, Inc., 1996.

Bulla, Joanne DeAmicis. *Images of America: Fords*. Charleston, S.C.: Arcadia Publishing, 2002.

Butler, David. *Edward the King: Prince of Hearts*. New York: Pocket Books, 1976.

Canfield, Leon H. and Howard B. Wilder. *The Making of Modern America*. Boston: Houghton Mifflin Company, 1956.

Cawley, James and Margaret. *Exploring the Little Rivers of New Jersey*. Princeton, N.J.: Princeton University Press, 1942.

Cunningham, John T. *New Jersey: America's Main Road*. Garden City, N.Y.: Doubleday and Company, 1966.

– – – – – – – – . *Newark*. Newark, N.J.: The New Jersey Historical Society, 1966.

Derry, Ellis L. *Old and Historic Churches of New Jersey*. Union City, N.J.: Wm. H. Wise & Co., Inc., 1979.

Desmond, Helen, ed. *From the Passaiack to the Wach Unks: A History of the Township of Berkeley Heights, N.J.* Berkeley Heights, N.J.: The Historical Society of Berkeley Heights, 1977.

Di Ionno, Mark. *A Guide to New Jersey's Revolutionary War Trail for Families and History Buffs*. New Brunswick, N.J.: Rutgers University Press, 2000.

Dillard, Maud Esther. *An Album of New Netherland: Dutch Colonial Antiques and Architecture*. New York: Bramhall House, 1963.

Doherty, Jane. *Awakening the Mystic Gift: The Surprising Truth About What It Means to Be Psychic*. New Brunswick, N.J.: Hummel and Solvarr Publishing, 2005.

Fallen, Anne-Catherine, ed. *Washington National Cathedral*. Washington, D.C.: Washington National Cathedral, 1995.

Farner, Thomas P. *New Jersey in History: Fighting to Be Heard*. Harvey Cedars, N.J.: Down the Shore Publishing Corp., 1996.

Gerlach, Larry R., *William Franklin: New Jersey's Last Royal Governor*. Trenton, N.J.: The New Jersey Historical Commission, 1975.

Greiff, Constance M. and Wanda S. Gunning. *Morven: Memory, Myth and Reality*. Princeton, N.J.: Historic Morven, Inc., 2004.

Groff, Sibyl McC. *New Jersey's Historic Houses: A Guide to Homes Open to the Public*. Cranbury, N.J.: A.S. Barnes and Co., Inc., 1971.

Hall, Walter Phelps, and Robert Greenhalgh Albion. *A History of England and the British Empire*. Boston: Ginn and Company, 1937.

Howe, Henry F. *Prologue to New England*. New York: Farrar & Rinehart, Inc., 1943.

Jones, The Rev. W. Northey. *The History of St. Peter's Church in Perth Amboy, New Jersey*. Perth Amboy, 1924.

Karasik, Gary, and Anna M. Aschkenes. *Middlesex County: Crossroads of History*. Sun Valley, California: American Historical Press, 1999.

Karasik, Gary. *New Brunswick and Middlesex County*. Northridge, California: Windsor Publications, Inc., 1986.

Konolige, Kit and Frederica. *The Power of Their Glory — America's Ruling Class: The Episcopalians*. New York: Wyden Books, 1978.

Krogh, Albert C. *Historic Perth Amboy and A Story of Odd Fellowship*. New York: Vantage Press, 1974.

Landreth, Sarah, and Francesca Romano and Kenneth Snodgrass, eds. *Historic Houses in New York City Parks*. New York: Historic House Trust of New York City and the New York City Department of Parks & Recreation, 2003.

Karabell, Zachary. *A Visionary Nation*. New York: Harper Collins, 2001.

Lefkowitz, Arthur S. *The Long Retreat: The Calamitous American Defense of New Jersey, 1776*. New Brunswick, N.J.: Rutgers University Press, 1998.

Link, Arthur S., ed. *The First Presbyterian Church of Princeton, Two Centuries of History*. Princeton: The First Presbyterian Church, 1967.

Listokin, Barbara Cyviner, *The Architectural History of New Brunswick, New Jersey, 1681-1900*. New Brunswick: Rutgers University Art Gallery, New Brunswick, New Jersey, 1976.

Long, J. C. *George III: The Story of a Complex Man*. Boston: Little, Brown and Company, 1960.

Lurie, Maxine N. and Marc Mappen, eds. *Encyclopedia of New Jersey*. New Brunswick, N. J.: Rutgers University Press, 2004.

Matthews, Prich, *Bedminster Township - 250 Years, 1749-1999*. Bedminster Township: Bedminster Township Committee, 1999.

McCormick, Richard P. *New Jersey from Colony to State — 1609-1789*. Princeton, N.J.: D. Van Nostrand Company, Inc., 1964.

McCullough, David. *John Adams*. New York: Simon and Schuster, 2001.

– – – – – – – – . *1776*. New York: Simon and Schuster, 2005.

McEwen, Robert J. and Virginia Bergen Troeger. *Images of America: Woodbridge*. Dover, N.H.: Arcadia Publishing, 1997.

McGinnis, William C. *History of Perth Amboy, New Jersey 1651-1960*. Perth Amboy, N.J.: American Publishing Company, 1960.

Miers, Earl Schenk. *Where the Raritan Flows*. New Brunswick, N.J.: Rutgers University Press, 1964.

Mitchell, Craig. *George Washington's New Jersey: A Guide to the Crossroads of the American Revolution*. Moorestown, N.J.: Middle Atlantic Press, 2003.

Mitnick, Barbara J., ed. *New Jersey and the American Revolution*. Piscataway, N.J.: Rutgers University Press, 2005.

Morrissey, Brendan. *Monmouth Courthouse 1778: The Last Great Battle in the North*. Oxford, United Kingdom: Osprey Publishing, 2004.

Peck, Donald Johnstone, and Frank Cahir, Ann Miles and Werner Ulrich. *History of Colts Neck*. Colts Neck, N.J.: Colts Neck Historical Committee, 1964.

Pomfret, John E. *The Province of East New Jersey, 1609-1702*. Princeton, N.J.: Princeton University Press, 1962.

Randall, Willard S., *The Proprietary House in Amboy*. Perth Amboy, N.J.: Proprietary House Association, 1975.

Raftis, Edmund B., *Summit, New Jersey*. Seattle, Washington: Great Swamp Press, 1996.

Rosenfeld, Richard N. *America Aurora: A Democratic-Republican Returns*. New York: St. Martin's Press, 1997.

Schimizzi, Ernest and Gregory, *The Staten Island Peace Conference: September 11, 1776*. Albany, N.Y.: New York State American Revolution Bicentennial Commission, 1976.

Shipley, F. Alexander, Robin J. Shipley and Linda A. Bragdon. *Rediscovery of Rahway*. Self-published, 1976.

Society of Colonial Wars in the State of New Jersey, The. *Historic Roadsides in New Jersey*. 1928.

Stellhorn, Paul A., and Michael J. Birkner, eds. *The Governors of New Jersey, 1664-1974*. Trenton, N.J.: New Jersey Historical Commission, 1982.

Sullivan, Walter. *Landprints on the Magnificent American Landscape*. New York: New York Times Book Co., 1984.

Thomann, G. *Colonial Liquor Laws: Part II of "Liquor Laws of the United States; Their Spirit and Effect"*. New York: The United States Brewers Association, 1887.

Trevelyan, Sir George Otto. *The American Revolution*. Vols. I-IV. New York: Longmans, Green & Co., 1899.

Weisberger, Bernard A. *America Afire*. New York: William Morrow, 2000.

White, Margaret E., *Early Furniture Made in New Jersey— 1690-1870*. Newark, N.J.: The Newark Museum Association, 1958.

Whitehead, William A., *Contributions to the Early History of Perth Amboy and Adjoining Country with Sketches of Men and Events in New Jersey During the Provincial Era*. New York: D. Appleton & Company, 1856.

Widmer, Kemble. *The Geology and Geography of New Jersey*. Princeton, N.J.: D. Van Nostrand Company, Inc., 1964.

Periodicals, Monographs & Brochures

225th Anniversary of the Second Middlebrook Encampment. Bound Brook, N.J.: Heritage Trail Association, 2003.

The Abraham Staats House. South Bound Brook, N.J.: The South Bound Brook Historic Preservation Advisory Commission.

Clarke House and Princeton Battlefield State Park. New Jersey Department of Environmental Protection.

Craig House — Monmouth Battlefield State Park. Tennent, N.J.: Friends of Monmouth Battlefield, Inc.

The Crossroads of the American Revolution: A Driving Guide and Map to New Jersey's Revolutionary War Trail. New Jersey Department of Environmental Protection, 2000.

Domestic Life — Sara Marks Stockton at Morven, Diary 1845-1849. Princeton, N.J.: Historic Morven, Inc.

Guide to Historic Sites in Central New Jersey. The Raritan-Millstone Heritage Alliance, Inc., 2003.

A Guide to Somerset County-1777. Courier News, Apr. 9, 2002.

Indian Queen Tavern — East Jersey Old Towne Village, Piscataway, New Jersey. North Brunswick, N.J.: Middlesex County Cultural and Heritage Commission, 2005.

The Legacy of the Jacobus Vanderveer House. Bedminster, N.J.: The Friends of the Jacobus Vanderveer House.

Letter of November 23, 2004 from Mrs. Robert E. Lee, IV, Vice Regent, Mount Vernon Ladies' Association. Merrifield, Va.: George Washington's Mount Vernon.

Metlar/Bodine House, Circa 1728. Piscataway, N.J.: The Fellowship for Metlar House.

The Old Dutch Parsonage and Wallace House. New Jersey Department of Environmental Protection.

A Revolutionary Time: The Guide to New Jersey's American Revolutionary War Trail. New Jersey Commerce and Economic Growth Commission and New Jersey Department of Environmental Protection.

The Significance of Washington Rock. The Township of Green Brook, N.J., Oct., 1994.

The Trenton Battle Monument. New Jersey Department of Environmental Protection.

Washington Crossing Visitor Center Museum. New Jersey Department of Environmental Protection.

Welcome to the Drake House Museum. Plainfield, N.J.: The Historical Society of Plainfield.

Beech, Wendy. "Thomas Mundy Peterson — First African American Voter in the U.S." *Philadelphia Tribune Magazine,* Feb. 1994.

Chandler, Marguerite. "Crossroads Update." *Preservation Perspective,* (Newsletter of Preservation New Jersey, Inc.) Winter 2002-2003.

Cheston, Mrs. S. H. to Helen Hamilton Shields Stockton. "Letter Dated July 9, 1899."

Shields Family Papers. Princeton, N.J.: Princeton Historical Society.

Dawson, George. "Scotland and Its First American Colony." *The Link,* Raritan-Millstone Heritage Alliance, Volume 5, Issue 2 (Early Winter 2003-4).

––––––––. "The Day the British Raided the Millstone-Raritan Valley." *The Link,* Raritan-Millstone Heritage Alliance, Volume 6, Issue 1 (December 2004).

Drake, Avery Ala, Jr., Richard A. Volkert, Donald H. Monteverde, Gregory C. Herman, Hugh F. Houghton, Ronald A. Parker, and Richard F. Dalton. *Bedrock Geologic Map of Northern New Jersey.* U.S. Geological Survey, 1996.

Gardner, Andrew G. "A Grand Design." *Colonial Williamsburg,* Winter, 2005.

Hartman, Dorothy White. *Joseph H. Kler, M.D., F.A.C.S.* a Monograph. New Brunswick, N.J.: Middlesex County Cultural and Heritage Commission, 1994, 1998.

Higgs, Lawrence. "Ye Olde Courier News." *Courier News,* Apr. 13, 2002.

Hitchcock, Ann, "The National Park Service Museums Centennial, 1904-2004." *AASLH History News,* Vol.59, No. 4 (Autumn 2004).

Matteson, Stefanie. "Tour Gives Revolutionary Perspective." *Home News Tribune,* Febebruary 20, 2005.

Mills, John K. "Ten Crucial Days." *New Jersey Outdoors,* November-December, 1988.

Sokolow, Jayme A. "Culture and Utopia: The Raritan Bay Union." *New Jersey History,* Newark: The New Jersey Historical Society, Summer-Autumn, 1976.

Stratos, Anita. *The Monmouth Battlefield.* (Jane Doherty Visits the Battlefield, February 7, 1999). Jane Doherty Website, www.JaneDoherty.com, 2005.

Wall, John P. *Chronicles of New Brunswick.* New Brunswick, N.J., 1931.

Index

About the Author

DONALD JOHNSTONE PECK is an alumnus of Earlham College, Richmond, Indiana, Class of 1961, with a major in history and French, including studies in political science at the Institute of Political Studies of the University of Paris, France, 1960. Graduate studies included French at Columbia University, 1961, and theology at Drew University, Madison, New Jersey, 1977.

Professionally, he is the President and CEO of The Clausen Company, Inc., Fords, New Jersey, a leading manufacturer of automotive refinishing products for the automotive aftermarket and Past President of the National Association of Autobody Filler Manufacturers, 1983-1986.

Non-professionally, he is a Commissioner for the Woodbridge Historic Preservation Commission, central region Trustee for the League of New Jersey Historical Societies, immediate Past President of the Raritan-Millstone Heritage Alliance, Inc., Somerset, New Jersey, a Life member of the Proprietary House Association, Perth Amboy, New Jersey and since 2003 President Emeritus, having served on that Board of Directors for eighteen years and for three non-consecutive terms as President, a Founding Member and past Vice President of the Colts Neck Historical Society, Colts Neck, New Jersey, and co-author of *The History of Colts Neck, New Jersey, 1964*, a member of The Society of Mayflower Descendants in the State of New Jersey, descending from Mayflower Compact Signers: Francis Cooke, Stephen Hopkins, John Howland, Thomas Rogers, John Tilly and Richard Warren and a direct descendant of Dr. John Johnstone, Proprietor of East Jersey.

A recipient of one of the first of the Episcopal Diocese of Newark Commission On Aging Lifetime Achievement Awards, in recognition of the many contributions to church and community in 1999, he is a communicant and former vestry member of Calvary Episcopal Church, Summit, New Jersey.

As a long-term preservationist, he has been actively responsible for restoring the buildings, gardens and grounds at Olde Stone Cottage, at the site of the historic Cutter Farm, Fords, New Jersey.

About the Psychic

JANE DOHERTY, a renowned psychic for more than twenty years, is the leading authority on psychic experiences. Widely recognized and respected for her extraordinary skill and sensitivity, she has been featured on Fox Network News, CNN, the Today show, Sightings, MCNBC Investigates, WB11, and in numerous publications, including The New York Times. In Woman's Own magazine, Jane Doherty was named one of the top twenty psychics in the world by Dr. Hans Holzer. She starred in the TV show Dead Tenants, conducted the 2008 official Houdini Seance, and has been heard on over 200 radio shows–including Coast to Coast with George Noory. Jane is the author of *Awakening the Mystic Gift–The Surprising Truth About What It Means to be Psychic*. To learn more about her visit her website: www.JaneDoherty.com.

About the Cover Artist

FRANCIS J. MCGINLEY is the recipient of more than three dozen "Merit" and "Best in Show" awards. He was elected to the New Jersey Hall of Frame of Aviation , 1991, and serves as President of the New Jersey Chapter, American Artists Professional League, Inc. McGinley's art is permanently displayed at the West Point Military Academy at West Point, New York, the British War Museum, London, England and the U.S. Coast Guard Station, Atlantic City, New Jersey. Museum exhibitions include the Smithsonian Institute, Washington, D.C., the Newark Museum and Trenton Museum, both in New Jersey, and the New York City Museum of Natural History.

The McGinley cover painting is of the statue of George Washington located at Market Square, Perth Amboy, New Jersey. The life-sized terra-cotta statue was a gift to the city from its Danish residents in 1896.